# american
# SCANDAL!

## THE SOLUTION FOR
## THE CRISIS OF CHARACTER

# american SCANDAL!

## THE SOLUTION FOR
## THE CRISIS OF CHARACTER

PAT WILLIAMS

WITH DAVID WIMBISH

## Treasure House

An Imprint of

**Destiny Image**® **Publishers, Inc.**
**P.O. Box 310**
**Shippensburg, PA 17257-0310**

"For where your treasure is, there will your heart be also."
Matthew 6:21

ISBN 0-7684-3014-3

For Worldwide Distribution

Printed in the U.S.A.

2 3 4 5 6 7 8 9 / 05 04 03

This book and all other Destiny Image, Revival Press, MercyPlace, Fresh Bread, Destiny Image Fiction, and Treasure House books are available at Christian bookstores and distributors worldwide.

For a U.S. bookstore nearest you, call **1-800-722-6774**.
For more information on foreign distributors, call **717-532-3040**.
Or reach us on the Internet:
**www.destinyimage.com**

# DEDICATION

This book is dedicated with love and pride
to my son David and his wife Shawvana,
who model character daily
while serving their country as United States Marines.

# CONTENTS

# FOREWORD

I'm urging everyone I know to read this book.

It's *that* important. And it's a great read too.

In the pages of *American Scandal*, my friend Pat Williams issues a call back to the principles that made America great. With boldness, clarity, and humor Pat shows us how we can change ourselves, our communities, our nation, and the world by incorporating into our lives "old-fashioned" values like honesty...duty...honor...hard work...perseverance...faith...and more.

For as long as I can remember these principles have shaped and inspired me. When I was just a little boy growing up in Eufaula, Oklahoma, my mother and father taught me that if I built my life on godly values like these, I could never go wrong. During the years since then, I have seen over and over again just how right they were.

These values sustained me during the pressures of my football career at the University of Oklahoma. They carried me through my time in the United States House of Representatives. Now, they represent the driving force and motivation for J. C. Watts Companies. They can anchor the human soul during life's worst storms, shine the light of hope when darkness surrounds us, and lead America back from the precipice of disaster.

Thank you, Pat, for saying what all America needs to hear.

J. C. Watts, Jr.
Founder and President
The J. C. Watts Companies
June 1, 2003

# ACKNOWLEDGMENTS

With deep appreciation, I acknowledge the support and guidance of the following people, who helped make this book possible:

Special thanks to Bob Vander Weide and John Weisbrod of the RDV Sports family.

I owe deep gratitude to my assistant, Melinda Ethington, for all she does and continues to do for my family and me.

Hats off to three dependable associates: proofreader Ken Hussar, Hank Martens of the RDV Sports mail/copy room, and my ace typist, Fran Thomas.

Hearty thanks are also due to Don Milam of Destiny Image Books, and to my partner in writing this book, Dave Wimbish. Thank you all for believing that I had something important to say and for providing the forum to say it.

And finally, special thanks and appreciation go to my family, and particularly to my wife, Ruth. They are truly the backbone of my life.

# CHAPTER ONE

# WHATEVER HAPPENED

# TO AMERICA?

*The spirit of truth and the spirit*
*of freedom...they are the pillars of society.*
—Henrik Ibsen

Is American society falling apart? Anyone who looked at news headlines the last few months probably thinks so. Here's a small sampling:

- Xerox Corporation announces that it "mis-stated" earnings by $2 billion.

- WorldCom admits that it doctored its books to the tune of nearly $4 billion and prepares massive layoffs.

- Adelphia, America's largest cable company, files for bankruptcy due to fraud on the part of the company's founder.

- Twelve of America's largest brokerage firms agreed to pay $1 billion in fines to stop a government investigation into whether they gave misleading stock recommendations.

And there's more:

- Samuel Waksal, ImClone System's former Chief Executive, takes the Fifth Amendment when asked about his questionable practices that cost investors many millions of dollars.

- Sandra Baldwin, chairman of the United States Olympic Committee, is forced to step down when it is discovered that she never earned the doctorate from Arizona State referred to in her résumé.

- George O'Leary is named head football coach at Notre Dame but released a few days later because his résumé contains lies about his educational accomplishments.

And remember Enron? Nothing like a little manufactured energy crisis to increase profits. The list could go on and on, but mercifully we will stop here. No wonder public confidence in America's corporate and political institutions is at an all-time low. Unethical behavior seems to be the order of the day!

Stan Deal, a professor of accounting at Azusa Pacific University in California, told the *San Gabriel Valley Tribune*, "The magnitude of what is happening now is unlike anything I have ever seen...almost unbelievable." At the end of last year, *Newsweek* magazine quoted Dan Ryterband, managing director of Frederic W. Cook & Company, as saying, "I have not bought a single stock in 2002, and I don't plan to in 2003 because I don't trust anybody. Who knows where the next scandal will come from?"

## Time to Fight Unethical Behavior

*Character is a victory, not a gift.*
—Ivor Griffith

America has declared war on terrorism, and although that is good, our society seems in more danger of rotting from within than of being overthrown from without. Consider this: In 1940 American teachers listed the worst problems they faced as talking out of turn, chewing gum, cutting in line, and running in the hall. In contrast, teachers in 1990 said the top problems were drug use, alcohol abuse, pregnancy, suicide, rape, robbery, and assault! And things have not improved since then.

There is only one antidote to the moral collapse that threatens our country, and that is to return to God-centered morality. As someone has written about today's world: "We have taller buildings but shorter tempers. We spend more but have less. We buy more but enjoy less. We have bigger houses and smaller families, more conveniences but less time. We have more degrees but less sense, more knowledge but less judgment, more experts but more problems, more medicine but less wellness.

"We have multiplied our possessions but reduced our values. We talk too much, love too seldom, and hate too often. We've learned how to make a living but not a life. We've added years to life, not life to years. We've been all the way to the moon and back but have trouble crossing the street to meet the new neighbor. We've conquered outer space but not inner peace. We've cleaned up the air but polluted the soul. We've split the atom but not our prejudice. We have higher incomes but lower morals.

"These are the times of tall men and short character; steep profits and shallow relationships. These are the times of world peace but domestic warfare. These are the days of two incomes but more divorce, fancier houses but broken homes."

Does this sound like the type of world you want to live in?

Me neither!

Back in the early 1980s, when I was general manager of the NBA's Philadelphia 76ers, I became friends with Dallas Green, who managed the Philadelphia Phillies to a World Series championship. Dallas was a big man—around six feet, five inches and 285 pounds—with a foghorn of a voice. In my mind I can still hear him bellowing, "We need *character people* around here!"

Dallas was right. That's exactly what we need: character people. If America is to survive, she must return to the godly morality that first built her and made her great. That is the only way we can save our nation, our communities, and our neighborhoods.

I'm talking about rediscovering old-fashioned honesty and integrity, about returning to the days when you could count on a man's word, when a handshake was as binding as a contract written by a room full of lawyers. I'm talking about taking the Ten Commandments seriously and acting out Jesus' command to love our neighbors as much as we love ourselves. In other words, we must return to personal accountability and responsible behavior—what the Bible refers to as "holiness."

Of course, it's easy to sit and point fingers at those whose unethical behavior has toppled companies and created newspaper headlines. It's quite a bit harder to examine our own lives and see where *we* might be falling short. But that's where it all starts. If we want to change American society, we must first change ourselves. Jesus put it this way: "You are the salt of the earth. But if the salt loses its saltiness, how can it be made salty again. It is no longer good for anything except to be thrown out and trampled by men" (Matthew 5:13).

If those of us who call ourselves Christians allow ourselves to be corrupted by the "non-ethics" of these early years of the twenty-first century, we will have lost our saltiness and thus lose our influence in a world that needs us so much. The apostle Paul said, "A little yeast works through the whole batch of dough" (Galatians 5:9). This true statement works both ways. We can either influence the world for righteousness, or we can allow the world to influence us for unrighteousness. If we allow the world's immorality and dishonesty to taint our behavior, we cannot be the "yeast" and the example God intends for us to be.

Are you ready to change the world?

# CHAPTER TWO

# A NATION IN CRISIS

*Character is power.*
—Booker T. Washington

It's a dirty, rotten shame. It never should have happened to a woman like Susan. And I don't say that just because she's a friend of mine. She's also one of the hardest-working people I know, a dedicated Christian, and a devoted single mom with two daughters. Susan has worked hard to make a living for herself and her two daughters. Her husband walked out on them when the youngest was a baby, nearly twenty years ago. Since then she has devoted her life to her girls.

They've never had it particularly easy, but as Susan approached her fiftieth birthday, she was finally beginning to build some financial security. Two more semesters and both of her girls would have their bachelors degrees. After years of living from payday to payday, she had finally been able to get out of debt and even put a little money in a savings account. What's more, her years of loyal service had paid off with a tidy sum in the company's retirement plan.

Susan wasn't exactly counting the days until she could retire, but she thought about it once in awhile. When the time came, maybe she'd even have enough money to travel. She'd always wanted to see the Grand Canyon and Mount Rushmore. Unfortunately, there were a few things Susan counted on that she shouldn't have. First, she took it for granted that the top executives of her company were honorable, honest men and women. *They weren't.*

Second, she took it for granted that her company was a place where loyalty would be appreciated and rewarded. *It wasn't.* And finally, she took it for granted that her retirement fund was safe. *But now it's gone.* It vanished into thin air—or more accurately, into the lavish lifestyles and deep pockets of her firm's top executives—along with the company that once seemed to be an up-and-coming giant. Tragically, the company that could have and *should have* been successful was driven into bankruptcy by dishonest, unscrupulous managers, who were motivated by greed and lust for power.

There was a time when stock in Susan's company was worth over one hundred dollars a share. Today it is being sold for next-to-nothing on e-Bay as a novelty item. It has about as much value as Confederate currency at the end of the Civil War. "I'll be fifty in March," Susan says, shaking her head sadly. "What am I supposed to do? Start all over? I never thought this could happen to me, especially not in America."

Tragically, it did happen in America. Not only to Susan but also to many thousands of other innocent, good people like her. How could it have happened here? This is supposed to be a country where anyone can prosper if they work hard enough. We are the land of "Honest Abe" Lincoln and George "I cannot tell a lie" Washington. Somewhere along the way we lost our moral compass and have been cast adrift on a sea of lies.

> *If ethics are poor at the top, that behavior*
> *is copied down through the organization.*
> —Robert Noyce
> Co-developer of the microchip

If you want to join me in changing this sad situation, pay close attention to these five challenges from author Greg Morris:

- I will practice what I preach, no matter how hard.

- I will live what I teach, despite the difficulty.

- I will be honest with others, whatever the cost.

- I will put what is best for others ahead of what is good for me.

- I will be transparent, authentic, and vulnerable.

Jesus said, "You are the light of the world. A city on a hill cannot be hidden. Neither do people light a lamp and put it under a bowl. Instead they put it on its stand, and it gives light to everyone in the house. In the same way, let your light shine before men, that they may see your good deeds and praise your Father in heaven" (Matthew 5:14).

Writer Cox Barefoot puts it this way: "At some point, someone whose opinion matters greatly to you will be paying a lot of attention to your actions. They'll be watching what you do and how you react. You may not be aware of it, but they will be looking for you to set an example because they need an example to follow. They'll be looking for a leader. Each time you enter a room, attend a practice or a meeting...in fact, every time you involve yourself in the life of another human being...you have an opportunity to leave a positive token of your own legacy behind."

It is almost impossible to overestimate the importance of character. I would go so far as to say that an absence of character is responsible for most of the disasters that have befallen the human race. Mankind's inhumanity to mankind—the result of a lack of character—has caused more suffering and pain than all of the national disasters that have occurred since this planet was created. Human beings have caused more suffering and pain for their fellow human beings than all the floods, earthquakes, hurricanes, tornadoes, fires, and every other natural disaster.

A lack of character can be destructive beyond our ability to imagine. On the other hand, character in a time of crisis can avert disaster and help to build a brighter, better tomorrow. There are many important personality traits such as intelligence, a sense of humor, congeniality, and creativity; but in my opinion, not one of them is as important as character.

My belief in this matter is reflected in a recent survey of senior female executives. A large majority said that character is the most important quality of a strong leader. More than two-thirds said it was wrong not to challenge improper ethical behavior on the part of a business executive, and half said they feel very strongly that a leader who has committed an unethical act should be fired.

I agree with my friend, Chuck Colson, who writes, "As you go through life, whether it's in the military, in your business, in the church, or whatever walk of life (and certainly in your family), someone is going to depend on your character more than upon your IQ." I love the following story because it says so much about the importance of good character in every area of life.

## A Test of Character

Many years ago a young soldier stationed in Florida was reading a book he'd picked up in a second-hand bookstore. He came across some handwritten notes—in a feminine hand—in the margin. He was intrigued and turned to the inside cover to see if there was any information on the previous owner of the book. Sure enough, there was the name, address, and phone number of a woman who lived in New York.

He wrote her a letter and was overjoyed to hear back from her in a matter of days. That was the beginning of frequent correspondence spanning several months. The two talked about trying to meet each other, but before that could happen the young man was sent overseas to fight in World War II. Even then, their correspondence continued—eventually evolving into a long-distance romance. At one point he asked her to send him a photograph of herself, but she refused, saying that their relationship should not be based on what she looked like. He agreed and dropped the request.

The soldier made it safely through the war and made plans to meet his friend at Grand Central Station in New York. They set the time and location, and she told him she would be wearing a red rose in her lapel. On the day of the meeting, he was waiting at the scheduled place when a beautiful young woman came walking toward him. His heart began to beat faster as he thought to himself that she was the most beautiful creature he had ever seen. He desperately wanted to see a rose on her lapel, but sadly for him, there was none.

Even so, the woman smiled a perfect smile as she walked past and asked, "Going my way, soldier?" He thought about following her—rose or no rose—but then he noticed another woman—one who was wearing a rose. She was what you might call matronly—plump, with gray hair pulled back into a bun. The soldier didn't hesitate for a moment. He immediately chose friendship over physical attraction, stepped forward, and introduced himself to the older woman.

The older woman smiled, shook her head, and said, "I don't know what this is all about, but that young lady asked me to wear this rose on my coat." She gestured

toward the beautiful young woman who had smiled at
him. He turned and was just able to catch a glimpse of
her as she went through the door and out into the
street. "She said that if you introduced yourself to me,
I should tell you that she'd be waiting for you in the
restaurant across the street."

As it turned out, the soldier enjoyed many happy
years of marriage with the beautiful young woman because he passed a test of character. Just like that soldier, you and I are presented with many tests of our
character every single day. An important question is:
Are we ready for them? Have we developed strong
character that will carry us safely through any temptation to do the wrong thing?

## Five Qualities of Character

Character is made up of many things, but I believe that the five qualities listed below are especially
important:

- Character is what you do when you think
  nobody is watching you.

- Character is how you treat people who
  can do absolutely nothing for you.

- Character is how you behave during the
  petty aggravations of everyday life.

- Character is how you react when the
  pressure is on.

- Character is deciding beforehand that
  you are going to do the right thing.

**Character is what you do when
you think nobody is watching you.**

*There have always been hard times. There have
always been wars and troubles: famine, disease, and
such like...and some folks are born with money;
some with none. In the end it is up to the man
what he becomes, and none of those other things matter.
It is your character that counts.*
—Louis L'Amour, Author

Many know this great quotation from the pen of sportswriter Grantland Rice, "For when the One Great Scorer comes to mark against your name, He writes—not that you won or lost—but how you played the game." Sadly, few seem to live by it. Imagine how you would feel if life were a baseball game, and you knew that every bad move you made was going to wind up in the box score in the next day's newspaper.

Just think of how much trouble it would prevent, if every time we started to do something, we stopped and asked ourselves, "Would I want this to be in to-morrow's newspaper for everyone to see?" Think of all the trouble that Bill Clinton would have saved himself and the Presidency if he had seriously considered this question when confronted with sexual temptation.

Perhaps you've heard the story about the pastor who dashed into the market at the end of the day to pick up a loaf of bread and a half-gallon of milk. He handed the clerk a ten-dollar bill, took his change and his groceries, and headed out of the store. It wasn't until he was through the automatic doors and in the parking lot that he discovered that she had given him a dollar too much in change. He looked back inside and saw the long line at the counter. "It's only a dollar," he thought. "No big deal. I'll tell her about it next time in the store."

He started to walk away and then realized he couldn't. It didn't matter if it was a dollar, a thousand dollars, or a penny. He had to do what was right. He went back into the store, patiently waited for the clerk to finish with her next customer, and then told her what she'd done.

Her face lit up with a bright smile. "Forgive me, Reverend," she said. "I was testing you, and you passed." She went on to explain that she knew who he was, and that she had endured some bad experiences that caused her to think that all Christians were hypocrites. "I just wanted to see if you really believe what you preach—and I can see that you do." She took the dollar back and said, "I'll see you in church on Sunday."

As Karl Day of the Family Research Council writes, "Character is returning extra change at the grocery store. Character is keeping appointments, being on time, honoring your commitments. Character is choosing the harder right instead of the easier wrong. Character is setting priorities that honor God, family, country, and then career."

One business leader I know told me that any time he's about to make a decision, he asks himself one simple question: "Will my mother approve of this?" He says that exercise has kept him from making many moves that he knows now he would have regretted. Sometimes he isn't really sure whether a decision is ethical or not until he views it in the light of his mother's opinion. If he can't possibly imagine his mother approving of something, he doesn't do it. I think that's a great idea. Ours would be a much better society if we all paused to ask ourselves, "Would my mother or father approve of what I'm about to do? Would my spouse approve? Or my children? Or my brothers and sisters?"

Of course, if you are a Christian it should go deeper than that. We don't have to imagine that people we respect are watching what we do because we already know that God is watching us at all times. The question I have to ask myself is, "Will God approve of what I am about to do?" If the answer is no or even, "I'm not sure," then I know not to do it. G. Alan Bernard, president of Mid Park, Inc., put it this way: "A leader not only stays above the line between right and wrong; he stays well clear of the gray areas."

Another important thing to consider is that, even if no other human being knows what you've done, *you* will know, and a guilty conscience will eventually get the best of you. As the old Hank Williams song says, "Your cheatin' heart will tell on you!" Theodore Roosevelt said the same thing, albeit a bit more eloquently: "I care not what others think of what I do, but I care very much about what I think of what I do. That is character."

**Character is how you treat people
who can do absolutely nothing for you.**

*Keep in mind that the true measure
of an individual is how he treats a person
who can do him absolutely no good.*

—Ann Landers

Ann Landers' twin sister, Abigail Van Buren (Dear Abby), added to the quote above when she said that character is also demonstrated by how you treat those who can't fight back. No wonder those two dear women were so revered and respected during their long careers as advice columnists.

Former President Ronald Reagan is a man who always sought to behave fairly to everyone. Peggy Noonan, who worked as a speechwriter for him, says, "In all the years I have asked people about him, I have never heard a critical anecdote except once. I loved it, because it was such a relief."

She goes on to explain that the less-than-flattering story came from a man who had been working as a waiter in a restaurant many years ago when Reagan came in for dinner. The future president, who was still best known as an actor, insisted he had made a reservation, but the restaurant had no record of it and the place was full. Even so, the waiter told Reagan that if he would wait just a few minutes, a table would be prepared for him. Reagan indignantly refused, berated the waiter, and angrily stomped out of the restaurant.

Noonan writes, "I was so delighted to hear this story. Reagan acts like a jerk...like an entitled star. I told the man the story seemed out of character for Reagan, and he said he knew that, but it happened. I asked if he'd ever seen Reagan again. He said, 'Oh, sure, the next morning, when he came to apologize.'"

She goes on to say, "I am still searching for an anecdote on Reagan that truly reflects badly on him."

Why did Ronald Reagan apologize to a waiter he would most likely never see again? Because whatever else you might say about Ronald Reagan—whether or not you agree with the policies and the politics he has represented—Ronald Reagan is a man of character. And people of character treat other people with respect and honor.

Think of all the people you might come into contact with during an ordinary day. Servers. Repairmen. The custodian in your office building. The parking lot attendant. The postman. The clerk at the grocery store. The lady at the dry cleaners. Do you treat them as your peers? Do you show them respect and honor?

I realize that we all get cranky at times. When I'm on the road there are days that I honestly feel I have exhausted every bit of patience and good humor I can muster. No, I don't always treat people the way I would want them to treat me, but I try. And the more I try, the better I get at it. As actress/politician Helen Douglas said, "Character is built daily by the way one thinks and acts...thought by thought, action by action."

John L. Beckley describes people of good character as "generous; not greedy. They respect others' rights, property, and feelings. They are kindly and sympathetic. They bend over backward to be fair in their dealings with other people." Wouldn't it be great if that's what everyone saw when they looked at us? Better yet, wouldn't it be great if that was what we saw when we looked at everybody else?

**Character is how you behave
during the petty aggravations of everyday life.**

*It is in trifles and when he is off guard
that a man best shows his character.*
—Arthur Schopenhauer

Anybody can be kind and gentle when they are having a good day. There's no reason to tell a lie when the truth is on your side. You won't be tempted to steal your neighbor's Ford Escort with one hundred thousand miles on the odometer if you have a brand-new Jaguar parked in your garage. It's no big deal to let someone go first when you're not in a hurry.

The true test of a person's character is how they react when they're not having a good day—when they didn't get enough sleep the night before, or when they have an upset stomach or a headache. Their character involves what they say when the truth is only going to reveal that they messed up in some way, when a slight "bending of the truth" is going to get them out of a difficult situation. You might feel differently if you were the one trying to nurse a few more miles out of that little

31

Escort, while your neighbor was tooling around town in that brand-spanking new Jag.

People of true character are better able to weather the storms of life. They don't lose their tempers when they're stuck in a traffic jam on the way to work or loaf around in the office all day because they know the boss is out of town. Chuck Colson hit the nail right on the head when he said, "Far from being trivial, minor tests of character are the best basis on which to predict future behavior." Jesus put it this way, "Whoever can be trusted with very little can also be trusted with much, and whoever is dishonest with very little will also be dishonest with much" (Luke 16:10).

I'm always amazed at how people act in traffic, especially during rush hour. They shout at each other over the smallest infractions, flipping each other off for no good reason and refusing to yield an inch. Can you imagine what a horrible place this world would be if people acted like that *all* the time? What if folks ran up and down the aisles in the grocery store trying to fill their carts before other folks took all the good products? Imagine how it would be if people refused to be courteous to each other when they were walking city sidewalks, if they yelled and cursed and constantly tried to cut in front of others.

I have no idea why driving brings out the worst in human nature. I just know that it does. Somebody who can't control his temper in rush hour might say, "Aw, that's just me. That's the way I am, and there's not much I can do about it." Wrong.

Someone has said, "Character is the sum total of our everyday choices." The great American philosopher Henry Ford explained it this way: "Life is a series of experiences...each one of which makes us bigger, even though it is sometimes hard to realize this. For the world was built to develop character, and we must learn that the setbacks and griefs which we endure help us in our marching onward."

Old Henry probably said that because he knew that the automobile was going to give all of us plenty of opportunities to develop character! After all, there's nothing that helps to build character like a car that won't start when you're already late for work, or getting a flat tire when you have to be somewhere in a hurry.

Financier Warren Buffet is another person who believes that character can be improved and developed over time. Buffet says that the qualities that make up good character "are largely a matter of habit." He goes on, "My old boss, Ben Graham, when he was twelve years old, wrote down all the qualities he admired in other people...He looked at that list and there wasn't anything about being able to run the 100-yard dash in 9.6 seconds or high-jumping seven feet. They were all the things that were simply a matter of deciding whether you were going to be that kind of person or not."

I like the way Andy Stanley, pastor of North Point Church in Atlanta, put it: "Character is like a tree. It doesn't develop overnight. It develops over a lifetime. You can't wait until the last minute, do an all-nighter, and expect to pass. The measure of a man's or a woman's character is not determined by a fill-in-the-blanks or true/false exam. It is an essay test, and the essay takes a lifetime to write."

**Character is how you react when the pressure is on.**

*Life is your classroom in which you are being tried, tested, and passed...Learn quickly that the setbacks and griefs you endure actually help you in your march forward to success. The world was built to develop your character.*

–Jack Erwood, Author

The apostle Peter was a good example of someone who revealed his true character when the pressure was on. He also showed us that a person can change their character over time. What a difference there is between the man depicted in the Gospels and the mature, bold Peter we read about in the Book of Acts.

I admire Peter for being the only apostle who was brave enough to ask Jesus if he could get out of the boat and walk on the water. (The story is recorded in Matthew 14:22-32.) However, as soon as Peter realized what an incredible thing he was doing—and thus put pressure on himself—he began to sink faster than a row-boat full of sumo wrestlers. He was like an athlete who falls apart in a clutch situation: like a pitcher who takes a no-hitter into the seventh inning, and then gets so nervous he can't get the ball over the plate; or like a basketball player who goes to the foul line with the game hanging in the balance and bounces two shots off the rim.

In Matthew 26:33-35 Peter promised Jesus that he would die before he'd ever fail him. Then just a few hours later, he cursed, swore, and declared, "I don't know the man!" Even so, Peter didn't give up on himself. He didn't quit. And by the time we get to the Book of Acts, we find that an amazing transformation has occurred.

In the Book of Acts Peter won't stop talking about Jesus Christ, no matter what the authorities try to do to him. They put him in jail several times, but he goes right on preaching the Good News. They beat him, but that doesn't stop him either. They threaten him—and he knows what they're capable of doing, having seen them crucify Jesus Christ. Talk about a man under pressure! But Peter has changed. He has grown in character and in faith. He has finally come to understand the lordship of Jesus Christ. He has completely surrendered his life and his will to God, and he has been empowered by the Holy Spirit.

This brings me to a very important point. When it comes to character, those who belong to Christ have a tremendous advantage over those who don't know Him. (Actually, those who belong to Christ have a tremendous advantage in every area of life!) That's because He gives us power and strength that are far beyond our normal capabilities. He enables us to stand when we'd otherwise fall, to walk when we'd otherwise be standing still, and to run when we'd otherwise be forced to crawl.

If you don't know Jesus Christ, I urge you to take a moment to meet Him. Just stop right now, wherever you are, and pray this prayer—silently if you'd prefer.

> *Lord Jesus, I acknowledge that I am a sinner, and I understand that the penalty for sin is death and eternal separation from God. I know, Lord, that You paid the penalty for my sin—that you were crucified in my place, and that I can be forgiven only because of your shed blood and only through faith in You. Jesus, I acknowledge You as Lord and Savior of my life. Help me to live for You from this day forward. Amen.*

Pastor Andy Stanley, whom I quoted earlier, has written, "The bottom line for all believers is that God owns us, and in order to become men and women of character, we must surrender to His ownership." He goes on to say, "Putting these two basic tenets together... God's sovereignty and His right to ownership...character can be defined in this way: Character is the will to do what is right, as defined by God, regardless of personal cost."

**Character is deciding beforehand**
**that you are going to do the right thing.**

*Decide to construct your character through excellent actions and determine to pay the price of a worthy goal...and one day you will build something that endures, something worthy of your potential.*
—Epictetus, Philosopher

If you live in Florida like I do, you'd better know in advance what you're going to do if and when the National Weather Service tells you that a hurricane is headed your way. I'm certain that those who live right on the coast already know the highways to higher ground, and they're ready to take them if and when a monster storm comes howling in from the Caribbean. There's not as much danger when you live as far inland as the Orlando area, but even there Florida folks are prepared for a hurricane.

In California a lot of people have put together earthquake kits, which include things like a flashlight, a portable radio, and water. You can never tell when an earthquake is going to hit, but they want to be prepared—especially if "the big one" strikes.

Consider the second baseman on a baseball team. He's always thinking about what he's going to do with the ball if it's hit to him. For example, if there's no one on base, he'll obviously throw the ball to first for the out. But if there's a runner on first, he'll start a double play. If the bases are loaded with nobody out, he'll throw the ball to home plate in an attempt to keep a run from scoring. He will also change where he stands in the infield depending on whether there's anyone on base, if the hitter is right-handed or left-handed, and whether the hitter has speed or power.

It takes more than a good arm or glove to be a major league second baseman. You have to be thinking all the time about what you're going to do next. I've seen some guys with great talent who never made it to the top—or who didn't stay there very long—because they didn't use their heads. In the same way, if you want to be a person of character, it's a good idea to think about how you will handle any situation or temptation that might arise. Make up your mind that you will do the right and honorable thing in every situation.

For instance, have you ever been at a dinner party when people started bad-mouthing or gossiping about someone you knew? Did you join in? I admit that I have. Afterwards, I felt guilty about it. So I have made up my mind that from now on, I'm just not going to get involved in that kind of conversation. It's not right or constructive, and I'm not going to do it.

Gossip may be one of the more minor sins, but I use it as an example of the lack of strength and character that has gotten this country into trouble. What I am talking about is deciding beforehand that you will be honest in all situations—even when you're dealing the Internal Revenue Service!

- Knowing that you will not steal or cheat, even if you have a friend on the board of directors of a major corporation, and they are giving you insider-trading information.

- Resolving that you will not cheat on your spouse, even if you're ten thousand miles from home, lonely, and they will never find out.

- Making up your mind that you will be as kind and gentle as you can possibly be in all situations.

- Being so honest that you point out to the waitress that she forgot to charge you for the dessert.

I am talking about standing up for what is right and good in every situation.

After his empire crumbled around him, televangelist Jim Bakker said that 95 percent of his ministry was in order, but 5 percent was not. He tried concealing that 5 percent, but it eventually brought him down. Character involves making sure that everything is as it should be.

Let's take a quick moment to recap what we've talked about in this chapter. Now you can determine your character by observing:

- What you do when you think nobody is watching you.

- How you treat people who can do absolutely nothing for you.

- How you behave during the petty aggravations of everyday life.

- How you react when the pressure is on.

- If you decide beforehand that you are going to do the right thing.

Certainly life would be much better for all of us if everyone demonstrated all of these characteristics. You may say, "Sure, but this is all kind of unrealistic, isn't it?

It's just not human nature to behave this way." My answer is that the very best way to change the world is to start with ourselves. As the old hymn says, "Let there be peace on earth, and let it begin with me." I truly believe that if we do what we can to be salt and light, the rest will take care of itself.

> *We must take care to live not merely a long life,*
> *but a full one, for living a long life requires only*
> *good fortune, but living a full life requires character.*
> —Seneca, Ancient Statesman

In the next chapter we'll talk about the tools we need to build better character—and thus a better world for all of us.

# CHAPTER THREE

# THE BUILDING BLOCKS

# OF CHARACTER

*Would you buy a used car from yourself?*
—Sparky Anderson
Hall of Fame Baseball Manager

Just when you think we're running out of heroes, three women come along and give you hope that things really can change. Their names are Cynthia Cooper, Sherron Watkins, and Coleen Rowley, and they are Time magazine's Persons of the Year for 2002. These women were chosen for the honor because they stood up under incredible pressure and spoke out about improper practices by their employers—Cooper at World-Com, Watkins at Enron, and Rowley at the Federal Bureau of Investigation.

These women are not "tattletales." Each of them went to the top of their respective organizations in an attempt to get the scandalous behavior to stop, but all of them were rebuffed. It was only after exhausting all other possible channels that they went public.

It wasn't easy for any of these women to speak up when they saw what was going on. Cynthia Cooper said, "There is a price to be paid. There have been times that I could not stop crying." Then why did she do it? Why did she stick her neck out and put her career on the line?

"I think it comes back to values and ethics that you learn through your life," she says. "My mother has been a tremendous influence on me. 'Never allow yourself to be intimidated. Always think about the consequences of your actions.' I think this is a wake-up call for the country. There's a responsibility for all Americans—teachers, mothers, fathers, college professors, corporate people—to help and make sure the moral and ethical fabric of our country is strong."

She says that when she began looking into company accounting practices, Chief Financial Officer Scott Sullivan told her that everything was fine, and that she should "back off." She was afraid of losing her job, but that fear was secondary to the obligation she felt. It turned out that WorldCom had inflated its profits by nearly nine billion dollars, the biggest accounting fraud in U. S. history.

Watkins, a vice president at Enron, went to CEO Ken Lay about "an elaborate accounting hoax." His reaction was to seek advice from company attorneys regarding whether she should be fired—a classic case of killing the messenger. But as subsequent testimony has shown, she wasn't really telling Lay anything he didn't already know. She now says, "People I thought were my friends and I thought would support me backed away. They said, 'You're on your own in this.'"

Rowley wrote a thirteen-page memo intended only for the eyes of her bosses at the FBI regarding what the agency should have done—and didn't—to prevent the September 11 terrorist attacks. When her memo became public knowledge, some fellow agents turned against her. In print, Charles George, president of Former Special Agents of the FBI, compared her to convicted spy Robert Hanssen and called her actions "unthinkable." Interesting, isn't it, that it would be "unthinkable" for an agent of the FBI to do the right thing?

Rowley told *Time*, "I don't see any concrete changes that are directly attributable to my actions, but it doesn't mean you stop trying. And if I end up flipping burgers, come buy some."

I am grateful for heroes like these three, who were willing to stand up for the truth in spite of all the forces that were lined up against them. Sometimes it seems that, even though our society is making tremendous strides in science and technology, we are going backwards when it comes to a determination to do the right thing. It is becoming more difficult to find people who put the good of society ahead of their own well being. No wonder we have been rocked by scandal after scandal.

Those executives at Enron were just looking out for themselves when they kept telling their employees that everything was great. "Buy more company stock," they said. "Enron is healthy and looking toward a bright future." Meanwhile, those same executives were dumping their own stock as fast as they could because they knew the company was in trouble. Thousands of employees lost their pensions as the result of management's breech of faith.

WorldCom laid off more than twenty thousand faithful employees due to its own faulty (i.e., dishonest) accounting practices. In today's society it often seems that the rule is, "Every man for himself." Many corporate executives are out to make a buck without regard to their employees or the public at large. Greg Morris says, "Leadership is not about impressing people but serving others. Leadership is not about manipulating people but motivating them...People must come first. People aren't the means to an end. People are the end."

As I've said before, the best way to transform our society is to transform ourselves. Jesus told us that we have to get the two-by-four out of our own eye before we can get the splinter out of our brother's eye. In this chapter I want to think about some ways we can keep those logs out of our eyes. More specifically, I'm going to talk about nine very important words that you don't hear much about these days. I call them "building blocks of character." Some of them may seem like relics from the past, and yet they can help us put the days of scandal behind us.

The building blocks of character are values, purpose, duty, virtue, morals, ethics, honor, reputation, and conscience.

## Values

*In your personal life, you must live in harmony
with your core values and your unifying principles,
the qualities and virtues that you consider the most
important in yourself and others. The more aligned
you are with the good, the noble, and the true,
the better a leader and better a person you will be.*

—Brian Tracy

What is important to you? It may seem like an obvious question, but have you ever taken the time to stop and really think about it? Do you have a clearly defined set of values?

I doubt very much if those greedy executives at Enron thought that "making money" was the most important thing in the world to them. Yet their actions proved that this was true. They never realized they were so greedy until their world came crashing in on them.

Now I don't mean to imply that most American firms engage in shady business practices. Most have wonderful values statements *and* live by them. I think of AmSouth Bank, where I had the privilege of being the speaker at their annual convention a few years ago. Their basic values are summed up in this marvelous statement: "Do more than expected. Improve someone's life. Make a difference. Make time for people. If something's wrong, make it right. Do the right thing."

You could do a whole lot worse than to live by those rules. I also love these "Commandments" from Emis Communications.

- Admit your mistakes.
- Be flexible. Keep an open mind.
- Be rational. Look at all the options.
- Have fun. Don't take this too seriously.
- Never get smug.
- Believe in yourself. If you think you can make it happen, you will.
- Never jeopardize your integrity. We win the right way or we don't win at all.
- Be good to your people. Get them into the game and give them a piece of the pie.
- Be compassionate about what you do and how you do it.

Let me ask again? Have you made up your mind about what is really important to you? I've known men who insisted that their values were centered in home and family, but when young, attractive, women showed interest in them, they walked out on the families they said they valued so much. Like those executives at Enron, they showed that they didn't really have the values they thought they did.

Albert Einstein said, "It is essential that the student acquire an understanding of and a lively feeling for values. He must acquire a vivid sense of the beautiful and the morally good; otherwise, he more closely resembles a well-trained dog than a harmoniously developed person."

It is vitally important to know what is truly valuable in life, and just as important to cling to it with all your might. If you know for certain what your values are, they will guide the way you live, and you will be less likely to trade something of lasting value for fool's gold. Think how sad it must be to be an old man or woman, looking back over your life and realizing that you traded your spouse, your children, and your self-respect for nothing at all.

I believe that one of the reasons why some American businesses have gone off track is that they have spent too much time writing up values statements and not enough time trying to put those same statements into practice. After all, as John W. Gardner wrote, "Only living values count. They must be reflected in actual behavior."

Of course, for Christians, our relationship with God should be the most important thing. Someone has said, "Core values are of no value unless they reflect God's values." That's a little redundant but very true.

### Purpose

*My basic principle is that you don't make decisions because they are easy; you don't make them because they are cheap; you don't make them because they are popular. You make them because they are right."*
—Rev. Theodore M. Hesburgh, CSC
Former President, University of Notre Dame

As I'm using it here, the word *purpose* can be defined in two ways. The first is "meaning," as in, "God has a purpose for your life." The second definition is "determination or resolution," as when Daniel "purposed in his heart" not to defile himself by eating Nebuchadnezzar's food or drinking his wine. (See Daniel 1:8 KJV.)

I want you to know that there's more to life than punching a time clock. There's more to life than spending five or six days a week at the office; or weekends spent working in the yard, doing housework, or watching television. There is a reason why you are here. God has something that you and only you can do. It is your *purpose*, and it will contribute to the construction of a better world.

You may ask, "Who, me?"

Yes, you!

Think about how unique you are. No one else has your fingerprints, your voice pattern, or your face. No one else has ever had your thoughts. It may sound a bit mushy when you hear it in a love song, but it's really true: No one else could ever take your place. And I believe that if you don't fulfill the purpose God has in mind for you, He'll raise up someone else to do it—but it won't be done as well.

Take the Old Testament character of Jonah, for example. God told him to preach to the inhabitants of Ninevah and tell them that they were going to be destroyed if they didn't repent from their wicked ways. As I'm sure you know, Jonah didn't want anything to do with the rough characters in Ninevah, so he ran in the other direction.

What did God do about Jonah? He sent a storm to blow against the ship on which Jonah was sailing, ultimately causing him to be thrown overboard. He sent a big fish to swallow Jonah, rather than letting him drown or be devoured by a less-friendly fish with sharper teeth. Then He had that fish vomit Jonah onto dry land, still alive and kicking.

Why did God go to all that trouble? Couldn't He simply have told another prophet to preach to the people of Ninevah? Of course! But for some reason God wanted Jonah—and Jonah alone—to do it. Perhaps he knew that Jonah would be more effective than any other prophet of his day. Whatever the reason, the only thing we can really know is that there was a purpose for Jonah's life, just as there's a purpose for yours and mine.

Do you know what your purpose is? Here's how you can find it.

- Seek God's will through prayer and meditation.

- Look for Him to reveal His will for you through His Word.

- Listen to the wisdom that comes to you from other Christians you have learned to respect and trust. (Of course, any advice you get should be weighed in light of what you feel God is saying to you through prayer and study of His Word.)

- Take a look at the knowledge and skills God has given you. (For example, if you're six-foot-eleven and weigh three hundred pounds, I don't think God is calling you to be a jockey!)

- Look at how circumstances are lining up. (The older I get, the more I believe in the importance of circumstances!)

Once you've discovered what your purpose is, purpose to do it well. Act as if your life has meaning—because it does.

### Duty

*Duty is a word that is in disrepute. It fell into disfavor as rights became exalted over responsibility in our society. It has largely become a "four-letter word" in the American mind and consciousness. That result is consistent with the mortal blows that are being dealt to fidelity, because duty and fidelity are close relatives.*
—Charles Crismier, Author

As Charles Crismier says, duty isn't a very popular word these days. After all, duty implies doing things that you really don't want to do. Duty is what motivates people to do things like serve on the Sunday School Curriculum Committee at church, accept the job of treasurer for the local PTA, and work in the concession stand during Little League games.

I don't have any statistics to back me up, but I believe that American people had a stronger sense of duty fifty years ago, when they had less leisure time. In the 1950s, they were more apt to get involved in civic projects, giving their time to schools, scouting, and benevolent organizations. It seems to me that the more free time we have, the more we tend to guard it jealously.

I recently read a study of charitable giving and was surprised to discover that residents of the state with the highest per capita income—Massachusetts—give the least, percentage-wise, to charity. Meanwhile, people who live in the state with the lowest per capita income—Mississippi—give the most to charity percentage-wise. It seems that people with more have a tendency to give less, whether we're talking about time or money.

I think one of the reasons we've forgotten about *duty* is that we've come to see it in a bad light. We think of duty as slavish obedience produced by guilt. When we do use the word, it is usually in a negative way. For instance, we may shake our heads over the sad state of the man who is regular in his church attendance, not because he loves God but because he has a sense of duty to God. We feel sorry for the woman who stays in an unhappy marriage out of duty to her husband.

When I use the word *duty*, I am talking about actions that are driven by compassion for others, love for God, and a determination to stand up for what's right. It was this type of duty that motivated the men and women of the New York City Fire Department to go into the World Trade Center following the terrorist attack of September 11, 2001. When they ran into those buildings, they knew they might be headed toward their own destruction, but they didn't hesitate.

No one would have blamed the firefighters if they had taken one look at those burning buildings and said, "I'm not going in there! No way!" But they didn't think twice about it. People were trapped on the upper floors, and those firemen gave their lives in an attempt to save them. In doing so, they showed the greatest possible love for their fellow human beings. Jesus said, "Greater love has no one than this, that he lay down his life for his friends" (John 15:13).

This kind of duty—rather than blind nationalism—is what motivates reasonable men to go to war in behalf of their country or to give their lives in an effort to liberate those who are oppressed by tyranny.

### Virtue

*They are only truly great who are truly good.*
—George Chapman, Poet

It sounds like a word out of the Middle Ages. A relic from the days when a brave knight would go into battle to protect a fair maiden's *virtue*. Nobody thinks about virtue these days—especially in a world where sexual immorality is encouraged and considered to be the norm.

In a hotel room not long ago, I was channel surfing when I came across a sitcom featuring a half-dozen or so of the hippest people you'd ever want to meet. (In other words, it was indistinguishable from just about every other situation comedy on TV.) At one point, one of the young men admitted to another that during his entire life, he had only slept with three women. The laugh track went wild with derisive laughter. The joke seemed to be that even though this guy was attempting to act cool, any adult who hasn't slept with more than three people must be the geekiest of the geeky. I guess that makes me a geek, because I didn't get the joke.

The Bible says that sex is to be confined to a lifetime commitment between one man and one woman. The norm should be one sexual partner, not three! Having said that, I need to add that virtue has to do with more than sexual purity. Virtue implies a right way of living, a determination to do what is right and pure at all times.

The Bible tells us to add virtue to our faith. (See 2 Peter 1:5 KJV.) It also tells us to think virtuous thoughts. (See Philippians 4:8 KJV.) This is because, as political commentator Russell Baker has said, "You are what you think." Every action—whether bad or good— begins as a simple thought. Murder is the end result of thoughts of anger or jealousy that were never brought under control. On the other end of the spectrum, selfless service, such as that rendered by people like Mother Teresa and Albert Schweitzer, grows out of compassionate thoughts toward the less fortunate. It is so important to exercise control over your thought life.

Have you ever heard the old hymn, "Take Time to be Holy"? It's one of those old songs we don't sing much anymore, but it has a message every Christian should hear. The third stanza says:

*Take time to be holy.*
*Be calm in thy soul.*
*Each thought and each motive,*
*Beneath His control.*
*By looking to Jesus,*
*Like Him thou shalt be.*
*Thy friends in thy conduct,*
*His likeness shall see.*

As former Indian Prime Minister Jawaharal Nehru said, "To be in good moral condition requires at least as much training as to be in good physical condition." He could have been paraphrasing the apostle Paul, who wrote to Timothy, "Train yourself to be godly. For physical training is of some value, but godliness has value for all things, holding promise for both the present life and the life to come" (1 Timothy 4:7-8).

It takes practice to live a virtuous life, but the result is more than worth it. Virtue may sound like an old-fashioned word, but as far "as" God is concerned, it will never go out of style. Charles Crismier, whom I quoted earlier, said, "Virtue is not a plague. Virtue is moral goodness. It is purity in heart, motivation, intention. It is morally sound behavior. Virtuous behavior is that which seeks the best for those around us. It is not self-serving, but other-serving. Virtue is the outward display of inward character."

## Morals

*To educate a man in mind and not in morals*
*is to educate a menace to society.*

—Eleanor Roosevelt

The dictionary defines *morals* as "principles of right and wrong," and says that a moral person is one who "conforms to a standard of right behavior." Some people will tell you that moral standards change from culture to culture or from generation to generation. Not really. Some things may change—such as the proper length of a woman's skirt and whether it is proper to use words like "pregnant" in public—but the basics remain constant.

I agree with Voltaire that, "All sects are different because they come from men. Morality is everywhere the same because it comes from God." I believe the Golden Rule distills all of morality into one little sentence: "Do unto others as you would have them do unto you." Other great teachers have taught their followers, "Don't do to others what you wouldn't want done to yourself." But Jesus Christ was the first to put a positive spin on those words and make them proactive. He expects us to actively do good for other people—in other words, to follow *His* example.

I am convinced that one of the reasons we have been rocked by scandal is that we live in a world that has turned its back on moral absolutes. We have taken the Ten Commandments and turned them into the Ten Suggestions. However, as Dr. Laura Schlesinger writes,

"The Ten Commandments aren't prefaced with, 'If you're in the mood.' Where did the American people ever get the idea that God isn't really serious about this? When did we start thinking that we could ignore His moral laws, He'd bless us anyway? God didn't give us His laws because He wanted to be a spoilsport. He gave them because He knew that living in obedience to them is the only way we can build happy, healthy lives, families, communities, and nations."

When Calvin Coolidge was president, people called him "Silent Cal." He didn't say very much, but when he did open his mouth, he usually said something worth listening to. For example:

We do not need more material development.
We need more spiritual development.

We do not need more intellectual power.
We need more moral power.

We do not need more knowledge.
We need more character.

We do not need more government.
We need more culture.

We do not need more law.
We need more religion.

We do not need more of the things that are seen.
We need more of the things that are unseen.

That was true in the 1930s and it's true today. As John Locke said, "To give a man true knowledge of full morality, I would send him to no other book than the New Testament." Amen, Brother!

## Ethics

*There is no such thing as a minor lapse of integrity.*

—Tom Peters

I got a good laugh recently when a friend sent me a copy of a *Frank and Ernest* comic strip that ran in newspapers on Sunday morning. This particular strip shows a sleazy-looking client sitting across from his even sleazier-looking attorney. The attorney says, "The question of right and wrong is very clear. I want you to cloud it up for me."

That reminds me of the story about the pastor who sat next to an eighty-something gentleman on a flight. The pastor was pleased to see that the older fellow was intently studying his Bible. "I see you're a religious person," the pastor said.

"Me religious?" came the surprised reply. "Oh, no! I'm a retired attorney, and I'm looking for a loophole."

Sorry. No loopholes. And yet sometimes even Christians want to know the least amount of proper behavior they can get away with. They think, "If he gets away with *that*, then surely I can get away with *this*." But God calls us to hold fast to an unyielding and eternal code of ethics in *all* areas of life.

Suppose for a moment that you're the general manager of a team in the National Basketball Association. In basketball, more than any other sport, one good player can make a tremendous difference in a team's won-loss record. (That's because there are only five players on the court at any one time.)

Suppose further that you have a player on your team who makes all the other general managers drool. They want him so badly that they'd give you just about anything for him in a trade. However, you know something they don't know: your star player has injured his back in the off-season. He's damaged goods. If you trade him now, you can get two or maybe even three good young players with plenty of potential. If you wait, everyone's going to find out that the star is hurting, and then he won't have any value at all. What would you do?

I know that it's easy to say, "Why, I'd do the right thing, of course." But let me tell you from personal experience that it's not that easy—especially in professional sports, where winning is all-important. If the team doesn't win, the fans don't come. If the fans don't come, the team loses revenue. If the team loses money—or too much of it, anyway—you're likely to be sitting out in front of the arena selling pencils from a hat next season. I'm exaggerating just a little, but my point is that you're not going to hold onto your job very long if your team's not winning. If you don't get rid of Mr. Star, your team will have to eat the rest of his contract, which may amount to many millions of dollars.

Now that you know more of the details, what would you do? Would you really put your job on the line to stand up for what's right? There are people who say you'd be crazy to do something like that. They would tell you that this is a dog-eat-dog world, that it's everyone for themselves out there, and that it's your own bottom line that matters the most. They might even tell you that right and wrong are abstract ideas that change over time.

I wouldn't listen to them because I firmly believe that there is an excellent reason for me to do the right thing at all times, no matter what it costs me. That reason is my faith in Jesus Christ and my determination to follow the ethical principals He taught. I do not believe that ethics change with the situation or the century. I do not believe in following one set of ethics when I'm in the office and another when I'm at home.

I agree with this statement from *Life at Work Journal*: "True ethical convictions are not rooted in preference or opinions. They're founded on biblical standards. To maintain an ethical edge, we must shore up our understanding of Scripture; to find out what God says about such things as right and wrong, honesty, fairness, and treating people well."

A few years ago I read about a group of nine printers who walked off the job after the company they worked for took on a new client—a pornographic magazine. The men were Christians, and the magazine was contrary to their ethical standards. The company said, "If you walk out, you're fired." The men walked off the job anyway and, true to its word, the company fired them. I wish I could tell you that those men made the company think twice about its decision to print the magazine and that they were all hired back at a higher hourly rate, but that's not what happened. Instead, the company hired other printers to replace them and went on without them. This life isn't always like a movie with a happy ending. Doing the ethical thing can hurt you, at least temporarily.

My personal ethics aren't rooted in this world but in the world beyond this one. I urge you to do what I do: strive to keep an eternal perspective and rest easy. When the pressures or the temptations are getting to you, take a deep breath and spend some time thinking about who you are and what you believe in. Then act accordingly. Making the right decision may not benefit you right now, but rest assured that someday God will make it all work out. If He knows you've done the right thing, and you know you've done the right thing, then it really doesn't matter what anybody else thinks.

Let me share a little secret I've learned over the years. If you have to make a yes-or-no-decision and you're not sure which way you should go, your answer should be no. It's much easier to change a no to a yes than the other way around.

### Honor

*Success without honor is an unseasoned dish.*
*It will satisfy your hunger, but it won't taste good.*
—Joe Paterno, Football Coach

Honor is another good word that has become tainted over time. When some people hear the word *honor*, they think of two men facing off in a deadly duel for no reason at all—except that their honor would be at stake if they didn't try to blow each other's brains out. That's not honor. That's stubbornness and stupidity!

- In my opinion, a person of honor is someone who:
- Always takes the high road.
- Strives to be *con*structive instead of *de*structive in every situation.
- Is quick to say "I'm sorry," when they have done something wrong.
- Really listens to the other person's point of view.
- Is considerate of other people's feelings.
- Doesn't feel the need to have the last word in every discussion.
- Can be counted on to tell the truth at all times.
- You can trust with a secret.
- Proves to be a trusted friend, a valuable employee, and an excellent neighbor.
- Knows the value of hard work and perseverance.
- Doesn't quit or take the easy way out when the going gets tough.

You can see why honor is more important than ever in these turbulent times. There is an old Welsh proverb that says, "Be honorable with yourself if you wish to associate with honorable people." Smart people, those Welsh.

### Reputation

*It takes twenty years to build a reputation and five minutes to ruin it. If you think about that, you'll do things differently.*
—Warren Buffet, Financier

In April 2002 I competed in the 106th Boston Marathon. I say "competed," but that's not really what I did. I didn't have any illusions about crossing the finish line anywhere near the top of the pack. I run in marathons for several reasons: (1) because I have so much fun; (2) because running is an excellent way to stay fit; and, (3) because I meet such interesting people. (Actually, I don't do that badly for a guy who's experienced the trials and tribulations of raising nineteen children.)

That year I had the privilege of meeting Bob Kraft. He owns the New England Patriots, winners of the 2002 Super Bowl. I told him who I was and said, "It's a real pleasure to meet you." He smiled as he shook my hand and said, "Likewise." Then, as I started to walk away, he took one step toward me and said, "You have a nice reputation."

That meant a great deal to me because I know that it takes a lifetime of hard work to build a reputation. And yet, as Warren Buffet says, it takes only a few minutes to destroy one. Once you've been caught in a lie, people will never again think of you as an honest person.

If you're honest in your business dealings nine hundred ninety-nine times out a thousand, it's that one-in-a-thousand slip-up that people will remember.

One of the best explanations I've ever heard about fouling up a good reputation came from a business executive who grew up in Louisiana. He said that when he was a boy, he often went fishing with his uncle. "He loaded up a big old washtub with ice and put our drinks in there to keep them cold. I figured that tub was a good place to keep my fish cold too. So when I caught a fish, I'd throw it into the ice tub with the drinks."

Later on when he grew thirsty, he discovered, "My soda pop was oily and it smelled like fish. I scrubbed it good, but it didn't help. Finally my uncle said, 'Give it up, son. Once something touches fish, it has the smell and feel of them forever.'" The storyteller went on to say, "That goes for behavior, too. It's just like my bottle of pop. You can't get rid of that smell and feel no matter how hard you scrub."

That story helps to explain why I'm so proud of my good reputation, and why I do everything I can to guard it. I don't believe that thinking about your reputation is vain. The Bible tells us to avoid even the appearance of evil. If everyone was concerned about what other people thought of them, we wouldn't be reading about all these scandals in the newspaper every day.

I've heard it said that reputation is only a shadow, whereas character is the real thing. It's true that there are some phonies who aren't really what they seem to be. People have been "getting away with murder" almost since the beginning of time. They're what we used to call "Teflon people." Nothing sticks to them. But they are the rare exception, especially in the twenty-first century, when everybody loves to see everyone else's dirty laundry, and the media is more than happy to show it to us. For that reason, I tend to think of a person's reputation as being more of a reflection than a shadow. If their rep is good, it's probably deserved. Socrates said, "The way to gain a good reputation is to endeavor to be what you desire to appear."

Each time you are faced with a moral dilemma, I urge you to do three things:

1. Take the time to stop and think about it.

2. Pray about it.

3. Ask yourself if the people you admire, respect, and love would agree with what you're about to do.

The Bible says, "A good name is more desirable than great riches; to be esteemed is better than silver or gold" (Proverbs 22:1). James Preston, the CEO of Avon Products, comes at it from the opposite direction. "A bad reputation is like a hangover," he says. "It takes a while to get rid of, and it makes everything else hurt."

Either way, the message is the same: Guard your reputation! Or, as Mark Twain said, "Always do right. This will gratify some people and astonish the rest."

## Conscience

*When I do good, I feel good. When I do bad,*
*I feel bad, and that's my religion.*
—Abraham Lincoln

John Wooden is one of my heroes. Not just because he will go down in history as one of the greatest college basketball coaches of all time, but because he is an all-around good guy. Coach was someone who never sacrificed his principles in order to achieve success. Now in his nineties, he remains an enthusiastic man who loves to pass along the benefit of his wisdom and experience. I feel privileged to count him among my friends.

At his ninetieth birthday celebration, someone asked him, "Coach, tell me your secret for a long, happy life." He laughed and said the same thing he'd said many times before: "There is no pillow as soft as a clear conscience." In other words, as he looks back over his life, he sees very few reasons for regret.

Someone has said that when a man won't listen to his conscience, it's because he doesn't want to listen to a total stranger. I believe a lot of men and women in this country have been avoiding listening to their consciences. Otherwise, we wouldn't be in such a mess!

We may not always think so, but the human conscience is one of God's great gifts to mankind. It helps to separate human beings from the animals. Animals don't have consciences. You'll never turn on the Discovery Channel and see a couple of lions feeling guilty about ganging up on a defenseless zebra. You're not going to see a cat hanging his head in shame because he can't stay away from the catnip. And your dog's never going to come to you and apologize for digging a hole in the yard. (Yes, I've seen dogs *act* guilty when they know they've done something that's going to bring a sharp word or a swat on the nose with the newspaper, but that's all it is: an act!)

Since our conscience is one of the qualities that make us better than the animals, it follows that people who refuse to listen to their consciences become more like animals. Unfortunately, the sharpness of the human conscience can be diminished over time. The more wrong actions we take, the easier it becomes to do wrong.

As I write this book, two men are awaiting trial on charges that they shot and killed ten people in the Washington D.C. area, apparently just because they felt like doing it. They are also charged with several other shootings, including murders in Alabama, Louisiana, and another one in Washington State. How in the world could anyone do such a thing? To me, these two snipers represent how far human beings can fall when their "consciences have been seared as with a hot iron" (1 Timothy 4:2).

I realize that the human conscience isn't a perfect guide. Some people's consciences are so sensitive that they feel guilty about *everything*. Personally, I'd prefer to err on the side of having too much of a conscience rather than too little. Besides, the Bible urges us to behave "with gentleness and respect, keeping a clear conscience so that those who speak maliciously of your behavior in Christ may be ashamed of their slander" (1 Peter 3:16).

Have you ever heard of Hansen's Disease? It also goes by the name of leprosy. People who have this illness do not feel any pain in their extremities. A woman with Hansen's Disease would never know if she stepped on a sharp piece of glass. A man wouldn't feel it if he laid his hand on a hot stove. As a result, people who have this disease eventually become deformed and crippled. Their fingers and toes are broken and gnarled. They get to the point where they cannot walk or use their hands, all because they cannot feel pain.

Physical pain protects the body, and the pain inflicted by a tender conscience protects the spirit. So pay attention to your conscience. Always remember that God gave it to you for a reason.

# CHAPTER FOUR

# SEARCHING FOR

# AN HONEST MAN

*Honesty is better than all policy.*
—Immanuel Kant

I wonder if Diogenes is still out there somewhere, carrying that lantern. According to the ancient Greek legend, Diogenes spent his time searching the world for an honest man. Even though he carried that ancient "flashlight" with him, he couldn't seem to find what he was looking for. Poor Digoenes! If he couldn't find an honest man in ancient Greece, he would certainly be hard-pressed to find one in modern America.

Or *maybe not*. There's one in Florida, although he's not exactly a man. His name is Jawanza Jones, he's eight years old, and he lives in Gainesville. He and his mom spend their nights in a homeless shelter called St. Francis House. Not long ago Jawanza found a wallet on the floor of a grocery store restroom. When he picked it up, he saw that it had a number of credit cards in it, along with something else that might be even more tempting to a homeless boy and his mother: cash consisting of three twenty-dollar bills.

Sixty dollars may not seem like a tremendous amount of money to you or me, but imagine what a fortune it would be if you were eight years old and homeless. It could buy a whole bunch of hamburgers or hotdogs for a hungry boy—not to mention candy bars, chips, and soda. Be that as it may, Jawanza is an honest young man, so he and his mother turned in the wallet to the manager of the grocery store, who notified the man who lost it.

I'm happy to tell you that Jawanza's honesty was rewarded. When the owner got his wallet back, he gave the boy a fifteen-dollar reward. Then, when a reporter asked him what he was going to do with his money, Jawanza replied that he was saving it because he wanted to buy a bicycle. The very next day someone showed up at the homeless shelter with a shiny new bike for him.

Over the next few days Jawanza's mother received a number of phone calls offering other help, including an apartment at reduced rent until she could get her life back on track. "I've gotten calls from everywhere," she said.

I'm delighted that a little boy's honesty was reinforced in so many positive ways, but Jawanza didn't know all this was going to happen when he turned in that billfold. The sad truth is that honesty isn't always rewarded. If being honest always brought good results, just about everyone would be honest all the time.

It doesn't work that way. As you and I both know, being honest can get you into trouble from saying things that other people don't want to hear. It can make you seem dull and ordinary next to those who inflate their résumés and lie about all the amazing things they've done. It can cost you money when you insist on paying the full price for something instead of cheating and cutting corners. It can cause other people to laugh at you or disrespect you when you won't join in their schemes to save a few dollars.

A friend recently told me about getting herself into a bit of a controversy by refusing to let her teenage daughter use another girl's frequent-flyer pass so she could go on a trip with her best friend's family. The problem arose because the pass was nontransferable. The woman's daughter would have had to lie to the airline about who she was and even try to use the other girl's photo I.D. The mother refused to be dishonest not only because she didn't feel that it was right, but because she didn't want to send her daughter a message that it's okay to lie.

What kind of reward did she get for her honesty? An angry, embarrassed daughter, crying, "Why are you being so mean to me?" The ridicule of a "friend," who asked, "Why are you making such a big deal about this?"

"I tried to explain that it's important to me to be honest," my friend says. "But everyone just acts like I'm crazy."

What about you? Do you think it's crazy to be honest? Is it really important to be honest all the time? And if so, why? That's what I want to explore in the next few pages of this chapter. But first, let me assure you that I never want to come across like a know-it-all, or like I think I can tell other people how to live their lives because I'm doing everything so well myself. Not at all!

I've told a few lies in my life, and I've suffered the embarrassment and pain of being caught a few times. I've learned from those experiences that telling a lie is never the easy way out of a difficult situation. If you tell the truth, it may hurt for a little while; but if you tell a lie, it will come back to bite you again and again.

Another thing I'd like you to know about me—actually, you've probably already figured it out by now—is that I love to read good books, especially the Bible. For that reason, much of what you will read in *American Scandal* (and other books I've written) is distilled wisdom from other authors. Having said that, let me tell you one very practical reason why you should never tell a lie: SOONER OR LATER YOU'LL GET CAUGHT.

Jesus said, "For there is nothing hidden that will not be disclosed, and nothing concealed that will not be known or brought out into the open" (Luke 8:17). That reminds me of a note found on the margins of an internal memo during an investigation of fraud at Tyco International, Ltd. On the memo, which urged the company's managers to create stories to support Tyco's accounting practices, one of the company's executives had written, "Be careful!! I wouldn't want this to get out!! I would strongly recommend never to put this in writing!!" Hmmmmm?

Jesus also said, "But I tell you that men will have to give account on the day of judgment for every careless word they have spoken. For by your words you will be acquitted, and by your words you will be condemned" (Matthew 12:36-37). Those two scriptures alone ought to be enough to make us stop and think before we tell even the tiniest and whitest of "little white lies."

Several years ago my daughter, Sarah, got a lesson in honesty when she impulsively slipped a small item into her purse without paying for it. It was cool until the security guard confronted her as she left the store. Sarah has always had a good heart, and she didn't need what she took. Her foray into crime was prompted by the same thing that gets thousands of teens every single day: peer pressure. Later on, when Sarah thought about what had transpired, she wrote me the following note:

Dear Dad,

What I learned Monday night was a lesson I will never forget. Shoplifting doesn't impress your friends or get you into the "in crowd." All it does is make your future look bleak and give you a police record. It was stupidity in my case, and I regret even thinking about it. For, if I had not even thought about it, my hand would have stayed by my side...I thank you, Dad, for what you made me do, and I am proud of you and also love you.

Love,
Sarah

There's only one way to avoid being caught, and that is to be totally honest in everything you do! Sam Rayburn, a wise old owl of a fellow who served for years as Speaker of the House, once gave this advice: "Always tell the truth. Then you'll never have to remember what you said last time."

It's human nature to try to take the easiest way out of a difficult situation, and it sometimes seems that bending the truth would be the easiest way. But that's never how it works out in the long run. One lie usually needs several other lies to support it. If you don't have a near-perfect memory, the whole ball of yarn will come unraveled. Alexander Pope put it like this: "He who tells a lie is not sensible of how great a task he undertakes, for he must invent twenty more to maintain that one."

Sir Walter Scott said it this way: "Oh, what a tangled web we weave, when first we practice to deceive." That's true, and it's usually the person who tells the lies who gets caught in that web. I think of Richard Nixon, who was forced to resign from the presidency in disgrace because he lied about his knowledge of the Watergate break-in. I am convinced that Nixon would have survived that scandal if he had simply told the truth from the very beginning.

Then there was Bill Clinton's, "I have not had sex with that woman!" Certainly Clinton was guilty of immoral behavior, but he could have spared himself impeachment if he had admitted the truth rather than trying to cover it up with a lie. You just can't get away with a lie—even when that lie consists of not telling the *entire* truth, or when the line between the truth and a falsehood seems blurry.

John Adams, the first president to live in the White House, had this "prayer" engraved over the fireplace in the state dining room: "May none but honest and wise men ever rule under this roof." I wonder what John Adams would think if he were here today.

George W. Bush may have had this in mind when he said, "The role of the president, as far as I'm concerned, is to stand up and tell the truth."

I recently received a note and a newspaper article from a friend in North Carolina, telling me about a scandal rocking the campus of Gardner-Webb University. Gardner-Webb is a great little school, a Baptist college in the picturesque town of Boiling Springs. I have admired Gardner-Webb for years. I first heard of it back in the sixties when the school had a wonderful basketball player named Artis Gilmore, who went on to stardom in the pros. Then, when I was general manager of the Atlanta Hawks in 1974, we drafted John Drew out of Gardner-Webb in the second round. He too went on to have a solid career as a professional basketball player.

Since then I've watched Gardner-Webb turn out dozens of dedicated preachers, missionaries, and others who have gone into full-time Christian service. Students there are expected to attend chapel services every day. The student honor code is posted in every classroom. Anyone caught drinking alcohol or indulging in other immoral or illegal behavior will be expelled immediately. This is a place where everyone is expected to live up to strict Christian moral standards.

Following a campus-wide student protest recently, university president Dr. Christopher White was forced to resign—after admitting that he had ordered the grade of a university athlete be changed. The student was Carlos Webb, a star on the school's basketball team. He had received an F in a religion course because he was caught cheating. My friend told me that, according to university rules, an F received for cheating cannot be removed from a student's record. It must be figured into his gradepoint average. Although Webb retook the course and passed, the F continued to be figured into his GPA—keeping him ineligible for the team. President White was accused of asking faculty members to remove the F from Webb's record.

When this violation of university rules came to light, Dr. White said that he was just trying to be fair to a student who had received incorrect information. He explained that Webb had been incorrectly advised that if he retook the course and passed, the F would be removed from his record. Otherwise, he wouldn't have taken the course again. (There's that blurry line.) Dr. White said, "When we tell a student this is what he needs to do, we need to stand by that." He added, "They [students] deserve to be treated fairly."

After being restored to the university's team, Webb went on to lead Gardner-Webb's basketball team in scoring. With him leading the way, the school went on to win the National Christian College Athletic Association's championship. Webb was named Most Valuable Player of the association's tournament.

When word got out about what had happened with Webb's grades, most of the university's students were not happy. Absolute integrity was more important to them than a basketball championship. They protested for eight days, waving placards and calling for Dr. White's resignation. Eventually, they got what they wanted.

Dr. White, a minister, was forced to step down after sixteen years as the university's president. Even so, the campus remains in turmoil, and no one knows when the shockwaves will finally subside. But remember, revealing the truth did not create those shockwaves, but rather the attempt to cover up the truth.

Someone told me a story about a woman who came into a butcher shop at the very last moment of the day, wanting to buy a chicken for frying. The butcher only had one left, so he put it on the scale and told her it weighed two-and-a-half pounds. "Oh, I'm afraid that's too small," sighed the customer. "Do you have a bigger one?"

The butcher went into the back, came out with the same chicken, and put it on the scale again. "This one is three pounds," he said.

"Hmmmm..." the woman thought for a moment, and then her face brightened. "I'll take both of them!" You see, the truth has a way of coming out—always.

I like what Ellis Peters said in his book, *Brother Cadfael's Penance*: "Truth is a hard master and costly to serve, but it simplifies all other problems." I also like this from Tom Monaghan of Domino's Pizza: "I may not be the smartest guy, but I know how to be honest."

### Honesty Pays Off

*I think that honesty is still the best policy. I think morality still pays off. I believe in all those old-fashioned things because I honestly think they work.*

—Ann Landers

The second reason not to tell a lie is simply that in the long-run, honesty will take you further than deceitfulness—further in your career, further in your marriage, further in your relationship with your children or your parents or anyone else. Samuel Johnson said, "The first step in greatness is to be honest."

According to Andy Stanley, The American Management Association recently sponsored a survey in which fifteen hundred managers throughout the country were asked to tell which values or characteristics they most admired in their bosses. The most frequent responses were:

- He has integrity.
- She is truthful.
- He is trustworthy.
- She is a person of character.

In another study twenty-six hundred top-level managers were asked to list the characteristics they looked for in a leader. The hands-down winner was honesty. It finished ahead of intelligence, competency, and being inspirational.

I'm not about to name names, but I have known some people who tried to lie and cheat their way up the ladder to success. When I was younger, it really used to bother me because I thought they were going to get away with it. Sometimes I'd go home at night completely frustrated, wondering if I was the only one who saw what was really going on. You know what? I wasn't. If you can spot that kind of behavior, it's fairly certain that your boss sees it as well. I finally quit worrying about what other people were doing and started concentrating on what I was doing. I wasn't about to let other people's behavior dictate how I was going to behave.

I know from personal experience what it's like to feel as if you're running along on a treadmill, while the guy who's dishonest seems to be on the fast track. For a while their deviousness may pay off. He may be the one who gets that next promotion and the corner office that you deserve. He may get a bigger bonus than you, but take it from me, sooner or later a life or a career built on a foundation of lies will collapse. Honesty beats out dishonesty more than ninety-nine times out of a hundred, and God will take care of the other 1 percent. The Book of Proverbs hits the bulls-eye when it says, "A fortune made by a lying tongue is a fleeting vapor and a deadly snare" (Proverbs 21:6).

Author Robert Heller writes: "One of the least attractive myths of management holds that nobody can get rich without being a crook, a con man, or a mobster. Many crooks, con men, and mobsters have made great wealth. It does not follow that crookedness is the path to business success...Ponder, rather, how it is that the Quakers and other deeply religious gentry made so much worldly lucre. It was because they treated their people honestly and decently, worked hard and honestly, spent honestly and saved pennies, honestly put more back into the company than they took out, made honestly good products, gave honest value for money, and, being honest, told no lies. The naked executive can never find better clothes."

Legendary football coach Vince Lombardi, who turned the Green Bay Packers into a powerhouse in the 1960s, once said, "Skilled ignorance is often more powerful than knowledge and honesty, but only temporarily, only for a short time. In the long-run knowledge and honesty will pay off."

My friend, the late Dave Thomas, who turned a small restaurant into one of the world's largest and most successful fast-food chains—Wendy's—once told a reporter, "Honesty has to be my number-one ingredient for success. Honesty means being sincere. It also means being fair in your deals and agreements." Thomas also said that, to him, honesty meant telling "the whole truth" at all times. "Honesty doesn't mean hiding in the weeds," he said. "It means stepping out and telling the truth."

I love what Lord Chesterfield said about this: "Remember, then, as long as you live, that nothing but strict truth can carry you through with either your conscience or your honor unwounded. It is not only your duty, but your interest, as a proof of which you may always observe that the greatest fools are the greatest liars." Or, as Thomas Jefferson noted, "Honesty is the first chapter in the book of wisdom."

Noted psychologist William Schultz is another voice speaking up for the long-term benefits of honesty. Says Dr. Shultz, "If people in business just told the truth, 80 to 90 percent of their problems would just disappear." I would change that statement by taking out "in business."

I'm sure you know about the miracle of compound interest. If you have a small amount of money, put it in the bank where it gathers interest, and leave it there for a long time, it will grow into a large fortune. The growth is slow at first, but it picks up speed as time goes along and eventually reaches the point where it's growing rapidly. For example, if a distant relative of yours had put a couple of dollars into a bank account during the time of Christ, that account would be worth—roughly—all the money in the world today!

There is one thing that grows faster than compound interest, and that's dishonesty. Just think about this for a moment: The white-collar criminals of the early twenty-first century have gotten away with more money than all the bank-robbers from the beginning of time until now put together!

### Truth Is Absolute

*The truth is incontrovertible. Malice may attack it, ignorance may deride it, but in the end, there it is.*
—Winston Churchill

In George Orwell's *1984*, the government insists that it alone has the right to decide what is true. Big Brother's officials insist that if they say two plus two equals three, then two plus two equals three. But you know what? It doesn't matter how many people insist that two plus two equals three. It doesn't matter how powerful they are. In fact, it doesn't matter if the whole world believes that two and two are three. The truth remains the same. Two plus two has always equaled four and always will equal four! This is the truth and it cannot be changed.

This is what I mean when I say that truth is absolute. Truth cannot be created by wishful thinking, government proclamation, or a court's ruling. Truth just is. The late, great football coach, Vince Lombardi, said, "Faithfulness and truth are the most sacred excellences and endowments of the human mind."

"What is truth?"

Pontius Pilate wasn't the first human being to ask that question, nor was he the last. In fact, pollster George Barna says his research indicates that 75 percent of all Americans say there's no such thing as absolute truth. Taking it even further, he says that four out of five teenagers believe that no one can know for certain what truth is. No wonder, then, that more than half of all high school and college students admitted they cheat in class, and a third said they wouldn't hesitate to steal from their employers if they thought they could get away with it.

If there is no such thing as truth, why does the Bible tell us that God desires truth? (See Psalm 51:6.) Why did the apostle Paul challenge us to center our thought-life on "whatever is true" (Philippians 4:8)? Jesus even described Himself as "the way and the truth and the life" (John 14:6). He also said, "If you hold to my teaching, you really are my disciples. Then you will know the truth, and the truth will set you free" (John 8:32).

I believe in two types of absolute truth. The first is the Word of God. The Bible tells me that God loves me and that Jesus Christ died for my sins. That is the ultimate truth and the only foundation upon which to build a good life. However, I also believe there is an absolute truth in every situation. It may not always be what we want to hear, but it's always there. Sometimes we have to dig hard to find it; and once we do find it, even if it's not what we'd hoped, we have to be honest enough to admit it. As author Flannery O'Connor said, "The truth does not change according to our ability to stomach it."

I think of Lew Wallace, who wrote *Ben Hur*. He began working on the book with the intention of discrediting the idea that Jesus Christ was the Son of God.

However, as he researched the life of Christ, his attitude began to change. His doubt slowly began to melt away, culminating in the day he got down on his knees and surrendered his life to Christ. His classic novel, made into a movie that won ten Academy Awards—including Best Picture—became a wonderful affirmation of the Gospel.

According to his biographers, Socrates was walking along the beach one day when a young man came up behind him and asked if he could be the great philosopher's disciple. Socrates didn't answer. He just turned and walked into the water. The young man stayed right behind him, begging, "Let me be your disciple! Please let me be your disciple!"

Suddenly Socrates turned, grabbed the would-be disciple, and dunked him underneath the water. Of course, the younger man began to struggle and kick in an effort to get free, but Socrates would not let him go. After nearly a minute, the philosopher released his grip, and the younger man jumped to his feet, gasping for air.

Before he could even catch his breath, Socrates said, "When you desire the truth as much you desire air, you can be my disciple."

### God Demands Truth

*Thou shalt not bear false witness.*
—The Ten Commandments
Exodus 20:16 KJV

The biggest reason I'm careful to tell the truth at all times is because that's what God demands. I remember that whenever I'm tempted to take the easy way out of a tough situation and lie. I think about it when I'm tempted to hide something that ought to be out in the open for everyone to see.

Honesty is one of the many hallmarks of the Christian. If anyone is a follower of Christ, they should strive to tell the truth in *all* situations. It isn't always easy, and everyone fails from time to time, but anyone who fails constantly needs to reassess their relationship with God and ask for His help. As the Bible says, "We know that anyone born of God does not continue to sin" (1 John 5:18).

Baby Christians may lie and cheat, have immoral thoughts, and do all sorts of things that aren't in keeping with Christ's teachings, but someone who is more mature and has been following Christ for some time should be different. In any situation, I believe that being dishonest is a childish thing to do. Sometimes, when a child's imagination gets the best of him, he may not even know where the truth ends and a lie begins.

I wasn't surprised, for example, when a four-year-old neighbor told me that his father keeps a pair of wings in the trunk of their car. "When the traffic gets real bad," he said, "my daddy just puts the wings on our car, and we fly wherever we're going!" Excitement danced in his eyes. He was so carried away with his story that he almost believed it. He put his arms out at his sides—airplane style—and ran around in circles making zooming noises, showing me how it worked.

That's exactly the sort of thing you'd expect a child to do, but suppose his thirty-something father had told me the same story. I wouldn't have thought it was so cute then. In fact, I might have gone home and told my wife, Ruth, "Stay away from that guy. There's something wrong with him."

You have to be getting up there to remember the quiz show scandal of the late 1950s. I remember it well. Van Doren, who was a professor at Columbia University, became a national hero when he won week after week after week on the popular television show, *Twenty-One*. But then a disgruntled losing contestant told the press that *Twenty-One* was rigged.

Ultimately Van Doren appeared before a congressional subcommittee and admitted that he had been given answers to questions before they were asked. Most of the committee members congratulated him on his honesty. But not Steven Derounian, the Republican senator from New York. He said, "I disagree with the other members of the committee who have commended you for telling the truth. I don't think any adult, especially one of your intelligence, should be applauded for telling the truth."

Derounian's remark was met with thunderous applause.

Later on, when interviewed by reporters, Derounian told about the time when, at the age of twenty, he had overweighed a cheese shipment being sent by his father's business, and a customer complained. The future senator tried to tell his father it was an innocent mistake. "My father stormed back at me. 'You made a mistake and you're sorry. That's what every dishonest person says when they're caught. Sure, I know you didn't mean to do the wrong thing, but who else knows it? A reputation for honesty is one thing money can't buy. It can be preserved only by not making mistakes, not by making apologies. You remember that, boy, as long as you live.'"

One of my grown-up children has a part-time job with a company that seems to have a problem with honesty. His check always turns out to be smaller than it is supposed to be. When he asks about it, he's told that it must be a bookkeeping error and, "We'll look into it." My son says he has learned an important lesson in all of this, which is that it is important to live up to your promises. Otherwise, people will never trust you—and then you're toast!

### Always Tell the Truth in Love

*It is wonderful to have a high regard for the truth, but zeal for the truth must be balanced by a love for people, or it can give way to judgmentalism, harshness, and lack of compassion.*
—John MacArthur

I believe God expects us to seek after truth, and that He is pleased when we strive to tell the truth, as much as we know it, in every situation. The only caution I would give about telling the truth is that it must be done in love at all times. In other words, truth-telling must be balanced with a sense of what is proper and kind. Honesty is not an excuse for gossiping. It does not give anyone the right to go around harshly criticizing other people. The pursuit of truth does not justify sharing hurtful information that would be better left unshared.

I've known people who seemed to use honesty as a reason to be mean, and they seemed to enjoy it. If someone says to you, "How do you like my new dress?" and you hate it, what do you do? My own personal feeling is that it's less of a sin to tell a lie in that situation than to be unkind. Even if you think her dress is hideous, you don't have to put it in such blunt terms. On the other hand, you don't want to tell a whopper of a lie and say you think your friend's dress is stunning when you really don't like it.

If your friend is going out to an important event, and her dress makes her look like she just stumbled into town out of *The Twilight Zone*, then it's a good idea to tell her the truth before someone else does. Give her a chance to go change her outfit. But again, whenever you are tempted to tell a truth that might hurt or embarrass someone, check your motive and make sure you are saying it in love. After you think about it, if you're still not sure what you ought to do, turn to chapter 13 of 1 Corinthians and take another look at Paul's moving description of love. Then measure what you're about to do by that standard.

My friend Doc Rivers had a long, successful career as a player in the National Basketball Association, and now he's doing a wonderful job for us as head coach of the Orlando Magic. He's one of those people who seem to be able to get the most from their players at all times. When I asked Doc how he was able to develop such a good rapport with his players, he told me, "I just try to tell them the truth." He smiled and then added, "Players like hearing the truth, good or bad."

"Well, Doc," I asked. "How do you tell a guy that he's going to be sitting on the bench, when he wants to start?"

"I don't sugarcoat things," he answered. "I try to be respectful, to say things in a nice way—but I don't hide the truth. Even when it comes down to releasing or cutting a guy, I think that honesty is always the best policy. And the players always seem to appreciate that."

Yes Doc, I can tell they appreciate it by the way they play for you.

Let's take another look at what we've talked about in this chapter:

- Dishonest people always get caught.
- Honesty pays off, in every area of life.
- There is such a thing as absolute truth.
- God demands honesty from His children.
- It's important to "tell the truth in love."

Next up, we'll take a look at a kissing cousin of honesty: Integrity.

# CHAPTER FIVE

# DO THE RIGHT THING

*Let us so live that when we die even*
*the undertaker will be sorry.*
—Mark Twain

It was built nearly twenty-five hundred years ago, stands thirty feet tall, and stretches for four thousand miles from east to west; across valleys, mountains, grasslands, deserts, and forests. You've probably figured out by now that I'm talking about the Great Wall of China, one of the world's most imposing and amazing structures. It ranks with the pyramids of Egypt as one of the great engineering feats of the ancient world. I visited the Great Wall with a group of folks from the NBA about twenty years ago and discovered that it is even more spectacular than I had heard. What an amazing accomplishment!

During the time it was built, many cities were surrounded by walls designed to keep out invaders. (It didn't always work, as in the case of Jericho.) The Chinese were the only people to build a wall the entire length of their country. They did it to protect themselves from the barbaric and violent tribes who lived in the lands to their north. When the Great Wall was finally completed, the Chinese people breathed a collective sigh of relief and settled back to enjoy the time of peace they had earned, but that's not what they got. Instead, over the next one hundred years China was invaded three times—from the north. This poses a few questions:

*How could anyone get over that wall?* They couldn't.

*Did they break through the wall?* That was impossible.

*How about going around the wall?* The Great Wall stretches four thousand miles.

*How did the barbarians overcome this insurmountable barrier?* In every invasion they bribed a gatekeeper and marched through the gates.

*China did not suffer because of a breech in the wall but because of a breech of integrity.* That says a great deal about the importance of integrity and speaks volumes about the scandals that have rocked modern American society. For the most part our country's problems have come about because we've opened the door to them through a lack of integrity. It's an inside job.

This is why Ted W. Engstrom, former president of World Vision, hit the bulls-eye when he said: "The world needs people who cannot be bought; whose word is their bond; who put character before wealth; who have opinions and a will; who are larger than their vocations; who do not hesitate to take chances; who will not lose their individuality in a crowd; who will be as honest in small things as in great things; who will make no compromise with wrong...who are not ashamed or afraid to stand for the truth when it is unpopular; who can say no with emphasis although the rest of the world says yes."

## The High Price of Integrity

As a sportsman, I kind of resent the fact that two of my brethren are the butt of so many jokes about cheating. I'm referring, of course, to people who fish and people who golf. Unfortunately, I don't know any stories to prove that fishermen are really people of integrity. Hmm? But I do have a couple of pretty amazing stories about folks who like to spend a few hours every now and then knocking around a little white ball.

The first story concerns a guy named Jay Sluman. Chances are, you've never heard of him, and that's too bad. I think he deserves to be famous. Back in 1996 Jay was playing in the Bay Hill Invitational Golf Tournament in Orlando, Florida. On the seventeenth hole he hooked his ball into the water hazard. As the rules stipulate, he dropped another ball into a designated area. On the very next stroke, he put it into the hole. It was an amazing shot, one which gave him par for the hole and allowed him to remain just a few strokes behind the leaders.

That night Sluman took another look at the rules and concluded he had dropped his ball in the wrong place. He might have shrugged it off, but he didn't. Instead, he called the tournament officials and informed them of the rules infraction, which disqualified him from the tournament.

What's the big deal? The tournament's first place prize money of $216,000 was well within his reach.

My next story concerns a fellow you might have heard of, golfing legend Bobby Jones. Way back in 1925, Jones lost the U.S. Open by *one stroke* after penalizing himself *one stroke* for accidentally moving his ball a fraction of an inch. No one else saw him do it. He certainly didn't have to admit it. But he did and lost one of the world's most prestigious golf tournaments— and a pretty hefty amount of cash. When other people commended him for his integrity, Jones replied, "There's only one way to play the game of golf. You might as well praise a man for not robbing a bank."

I agree with Bobby Jones. There's only one way to play the game of *life*, and that's with complete integrity. But what exactly is integrity? My close friend Jay Strack says that integrity involves "realistic harmony of our talk and our walk."

Integrity involves honesty, but it's bigger than that. You might think of it as being transparent and completely without pretense. It is a character trait that the apostle Paul calls, "the holiness and sincerity that are from God" (2 Corinthians 1:12). People of integrity hold fast to their core values in every situation. They are like Abraham Lincoln, who said: "I desire so to conduct the affairs of this administration that if, at the end, when I come to lay down the reins of power, I have lost every other friend on earth, I shall have at least one friend left, and that friend shall be down inside me."

Alan Ross put it this way: "We usually confine integrity to the realm of honesty, but integrity is far more than honesty. Honesty is but one attribute of integrity. When I exhibit integrity, I am modeling the power of purpose in my life. An integrated leader is one who...lives up to a set of core beliefs or standards that are clear for everyone to see. The integrated life is the life of purpose and the life of passion. It permeates every aspect of your life, not just your work or family life. Integrity means unity of purpose."

I have been doing research for an upcoming book on legendary UCLA basketball coach John Wooden. As part of this research I've interviewed hundreds of people who know this wonderful man. One of those interviews was with a man who served as a student manager at UCLA during the years between the national championship teams of Lew Alcindor (now Kareem Abdul Jabbar) and Bill Walton. He told me, "There was only one John Wooden. The John Wooden at practice was the same John Wooden in the locker room. The John Wooden in the locker room was the same John Wooden at home. The John Wooden at home was the same John Wooden in the community." What a tremendous example of personal integrity—being "real" at all times.

Why have so many of the American people lost faith in our country's institutions and in the people who run them? As Greg Morris says, "Those people have substituted power, control, and manipulation for trust, honesty, and respect." If we are going to begin to reshape our country's moral fiber, we must begin "going against the grain," and that means living lives of absolute integrity and character. Anyone who wants to be a person of unquestionable integrity must:

- Understand that integrity is the only way to navigate safely through life.

- Talk the talk *and* walk the walk.

- Strive to be totally transparent and open at all times.

- Admit it when they make a mistake.

- Remember that integrity begins at home.

- Keep in mind that integrity is pleasing to God.

### Understand that integrity is the only way to navigate safely through life.

*As you are in private, so you are in public.*
*What is in a person's private life will eventually surface in public, for good or evil.*
—Joe Gibbs, former NFL Coach

One of the primary rules of navigation is this: *What's under the surface should carry more weight than what's above the surface if the ship is going to make it through storms without capsizing.* That's exactly how it is with integrity. What's under the surface had better be greater than what you're showing to the world, or you're never going to make it through the storms of life. A few years ago there was a television commercial that declared, "Image is everything." That's baloney! Even though our society puts a great deal of emphasis on image, it is really worth nothing at all unless you have something real to back it up.

Remember the singing group, Milli Vanilli? They won a whole bunch of Grammy Awards, and then the news came out that they didn't really sing on their records. They were hired because they had the image the producers were looking for, and that was the end of that. They had image, but no substance, and their musical career was over before those Grammies had been on the shelf long enough to need dusting.

That makes me think of a tough dog in my neighborhood, a German Shepherd. I love to run, and I put in several miles every morning and evening. Every time I run past the dog's house, he acts like he wants to eat me alive. He barks ferociously, growls, and jumps against his gate. He seems to be saying, "It's too bad this gate is here, buddy, or I'd get out there and tear you apart!" Well, not too long ago, he got his wish. He jumped against the gate and it came open. For a moment my heart was in my throat, but do you know what that vicious animal did? He put his tail between his legs and slunk back into his yard. He was terrified! The dog had absolutely no integrity! Again, image without substance is worthless.

Author David Ireland says, "Integrity strengthens you in your plans. A secure walk is a walk of stability, strength, and courage. It's a very peaceful feeling to move through life without having to keep looking over your shoulder because you're afraid someone is going to find you out. Integrity creates a pathway to God's promises."

**Talk the talk and walk the walk.**

*We have to take our boys and girls behind the scenes*
*of the world's work and let them see for themselves*
*the economic absurdity that any enduring success*
*or happiness could be built on trickery, fraud, or deceit.*
—Thomas Edison

In 1948 Harry S. Truman pulled off one of the greatest upsets of all times when he defeated Thomas Dewey in the presidential election. By the time Election Day rolled around in November of that year, just about everyone had given up on Truman except for Truman and his staff. However, when all the ballots were counted, the haberdasher from Missouri had won another four years in the White House.

A few weeks before the election, Truman called a meeting of his advisors and asked for their honest opinions as to how his campaign was going. There wasn't a positive opinion among them. Funds were so low that the Democratic Party did not have twenty thousand dollars to pay for several radio speeches the president had planned. After hearing all of the gloom and doom expressed by his advisors, Truman smiled and said, "Oh, I don't think it's *that* bad."

"Mr. President," someone retorted, "you can't run a campaign without money."

"Why not?" Truman asked. "We're doing it, aren't we?"

Almost as soon as those words were out of his mouth, the president was handed a telephone. A well-known millionaire was on the line. He had heard that the Democrats needed twenty thousand dollars, and he was willing to write out a check that very afternoon. However, he made it clear that he would expect some favors in return, should Truman win re-election.

The president wasn't having any of it. "You can contribute your money or you can keep it," he said, "but I'm not making any deals." Then he hung up. He didn't say a word to his staff about what had happened, but they saw it, and it had an electrifying effect on them. Seeing the president maintain his integrity when it would have been easy to take the low road revived their own morale. Somehow, they began to believe that they could run a successful campaign in spite of the difficulties they were facing.

The very next day Truman received a telephone call from another very wealthy man. "Mr. President," he began, "I heard about what you said to 'So-and-so' yesterday. You're the kind of man the country needs in the White House. I'm sending in a campaign contribution...twenty thousand dollars...no strings attached." Over the next several weeks contributions came pouring in from others who had heard about Truman's integrity in the face of pressure.

After the election, Truman and his staff could look back on that "strings attached" telephone call as the catalyst that turned the campaign around. Wouldn't it be great if we knew that all the leaders in our world today were men and women of integrity. All the government and political leaders. All the business leaders. All the community leaders. All the church leaders. Talk about heaven on earth!

In his *Pocket Power Book of Integrity*, Byrd Baggett says, "Integrity is: Doing what you said you would do, when you said you would do it, and how you said you would do it." When I think of all the people I've known who lived in absolute integrity, one of the men who comes to mind is the old singing cowboy, Gene Autry. Whenever Gene said something, you could count on it. That's one reason I had such mixed feelings when his California Angels won the World Series in 2002. While I was delighted that the team Gene built had finally made it to the top of the baseball world, I was also sad that he didn't live long enough to see it.

His widow, Jackie, remembers an occasion when Autry's attorneys wanted him to raise the price of a business he was selling by some $10 million. The attorneys knew that the buyer would pay that price, but Autry just said, "Can't do it. We already shook hands." No matter how much those attorneys begged Gene Autry to change his mind, he would not go back on his word. Stan Schneider, who was Autry's accountant for years, says, "Gene was always a man of his word, and business people knew...they were doing business with a gentleman."

Autry's integrity carried over into the character he portrayed in the movies. He insisted that Indians in his movies should not be negatively stereotyped, and he had other rules as well. His character should never shoot first, hit a smaller man, take unfair advantage of anyone, go back on his word, or advocate any racially or religiously intolerant ideas.

Boy! Wouldn't it be great if we knew that a bunch of men like Gene were in charge of things today? What a different world this would be. Instead, we have too many leaders like the young builder I heard about, who married the daughter of a wealthy housing contractor. The father-in-law wanted to give his daughter's new husband a boost, so he gave him an important job— building the best house possible. Money was no object. "I want it to be the nicest house this town has ever seen," he said. "Put the best of everything in it."

The younger man saw a chance to make some quick money. He slapped together a house that made a wonderful first impression, but anyone who took a closer look could see that it was probably going to collapse the first time a stiff wind blew in from the north. Most of Rich Dad's money went right into Poor Son-in-Law's bank account. When his flimflam job was finished, the younger man took the keys to his father-in-law and asked, "What do you want me to do with these?"

"Did you do the best job you possibly could?"

"Yes, Dad. I did."

"You spared no expense?"

The young man laughed. "You should know. You paid for it."

"Fine," the father-in-law said, holding the keys out in front of him. "These are for you."

"But I..."

"Go ahead. Take them. It's my wedding present for you and my daughter. You built the house for yourself."

A lack of integrity almost always comes back to bite you. The only reason I use the word *almost* is because God is merciful. Based on personal experience, I believe that God always wants the best for us. For that reason He sometimes allows us to get away with things we shouldn't get away with, simply because He is waiting for us to repent, change our lives, and be forgiven for our lapses of morality.

What if someone never repents? In that case, although it may sound flippant, I believe that sooner or later they're going to get what's coming to them. It may not happen in this life. In this world they may "live long and prosper," but I am convinced that judgment awaits.

God is not putting temptation in your path to see what you're going to do. The Bible tells us that temptation never comes from God. (See James 1:13-14.) Nevertheless, I believe that He does *get involved* in every temptation that comes to us. As 1 Corinthians 10:13 says, "No temptation has seized you except what is common to man. And God is faithful; He will not let you be tempted beyond what you can bear. But when you are tempted, He will also provide a way out so that you can stand up under it."

We have an adversary, an enemy the Bible describes as "like a roaring lion looking for someone to devour" (1 Peter 5:8). We are like mice and our enemy, satan, keeps baiting traps with cheese. Some people run in and grab the cheese and think they've made a clean get-away. But eventually that trap is going to snap shut!

**Strive to be totally transparent and open at all times.**

*When we speak of integrity as a moral value,*
*it means that a person is the same on the inside*
*as he is on the outside. There is no discrepancy*
*between what he says and what he does.*
—Billy Graham

Imagine what a great world this would be if you could take everything you heard at face value. What if you never had to think, "I wonder what they meant by that." What if you could be sure that every telemarketing phone call was completely honest and above-board. Maybe I've stretched your imagination beyond the breaking point. Just the same, it would be terrific if we could believe what the late Flip Wilson's Geraldine once said, "What you see is what you get."

History records that in the 1700s, Frederick the Great, King of Prussia, undertook an inspection tour of a prison in Berlin. As you might expect, when the king entered the facility most of the prisoners fell on their knees, crying out that they were innocent men who were wrongly convicted and begging the king to release them. However, one prisoner didn't join the others. Instead, he sat silently in his cell.

"You there," the king called out to him, "why are you here?"

"Armed robbery, Your Majesty," the prisoner replied.

"And were you guilty?"

"Yes, indeed, Your Majesty. I deserve my punishment."

The king called for the warden and ordered him to release the guilty man at once. "I will not have him kept in this prison, where he will surely corrupt all the fine, innocent people," he said.

You never know where you will find people of integrity!

In the 1940s Mahatma Gandhi was invited to England to speak before parliament. The invitation was something of a shock because the British had done just about everything they could do to stop this frail little man's fight for India's independence. He had been arrested, jailed, and threatened numerous times; but through it all, his influence only grew. Finally Great Britain's leaders decided to try something they'd never tried before: Listen.

Gandhi talked for two hours, speaking with great emotion and conviction about his country's plight and advocating her independence. The audience, made up primarily of people who had passed laws to keep the

Indian people in subjection, sat enthralled. When his speech was finished, the packed hall rose as one to give him a standing ovation.

Afterward, a reporter asked Gandhi's assistant, Mahadev Desai, how Gandhi could have spoken for so long and so eloquently without once referring to a note. "You don't understand Gandhi," Desai answered. "You see, what he thinks is what he feels. What he feels is what he says. What he says is what he does. What Gandhi feels, what he thinks, what he says and what he does are all the same. He does not need notes."

That's the way people of integrity are. They don't need notes to tell them how to speak, act, or behave. You don't have to wonder what they're really thinking or feeling because they're always up front about such things.

**Admit it when they make a mistake.**

*If we claim to be without sin, we deceive ourselves and the truth is not in us.*

—1 John 1:8

Somewhere along the line we've come to think that admitting to our mistakes is a sign of weakness. It's not. It's merely a healthy understanding of our inherent weakness as human beings. If perfection were attainable, Jesus never would have had to go to the cross.

The modern world's mixed-up view of integrity came home to me recently when a friend's daughter was applying for a summer job. In order to get the job, she was required to take a multiple-choice test to determine her psychological profile. One of the questions she was asked was, "Have you ever done anything dishonest?" Being a person of integrity she answered yes.

The next question was, "Do you think it is likely that you will ever do anything dishonest in the future?" Again, knowing her own frailty my friend's daughter filled in the yes circle. Bottom line, she didn't get the job because the evaluation revealed that she was someone of questionable character. Now I don't know who designed that questionnaire, but I wonder where in the world they got their degree—perhaps by mail order.

If I asked someone if they had ever done anything dishonest and they answered no, I'd think they were delusional. If I then asked if they thought they might do anything dishonest in the future and they answered no to that question, I'd say, "This person is a liar. I don't want him working for me!" As a wise man named Groucho Marx once said: "There's one way to find out if a man is honest—ask him. If he says yes, you know he is a crook."

The truth is that we all slip up from time to time, and when we do, a cover-up only makes the situation worse. That's what happened to the Arthur Andersen accounting firm. Theresa Howard, writing in *USA Today*, says: "Publicly admitting accountability early in the Enron scandal could have helped Arthur Andersen avert a federal indictment and the departure of its sixty biggest U.S. clients, experts say. Company executives stumbled by responding slowly to clients and trying to blame their Houston office, they say, and that left the company's image...and future...up to the Justice Department and outsiders."

She goes on to quote David Martin, the executive director of client services for Interbrand, North America, as saying, "It's eighty years of goodwill thrown down the drain in three months. It shows how easy it is to blow your brand." As we've noted before, a lifetime of integrity can be shot to pieces in a few unwise decisions. One of the least wise decisions anyone can make is to try to cover-up a mistake. It doesn't work.

**Remember that integrity begins at home.**

*I learned my core values when I was a kid...Work hard. Help the other fellow. When you make a commitment stand by it. Be tough but fair.*

—Michael Eisner

It has been said that charity begins at home. The same thing is true of integrity. The very best time to learn the importance of integrity is when you are a child. According to author Denis Waitley, one of the ways you can teach your children integrity is, "Let them accept responsibility for their own actions as early as possible." This is what best-selling author Kevin Leman calls "reality discipline"—letting your children see clearly that their actions bring specific consequences.

Waitley goes on to say, "Above all, for integrity's sake, teach [your children] graciousness and gratitude and how to share and care about the rights of others.

Teach your children that their true rewards in life depend on the quality and amount of service that they render, and that they should always treat others as they would have others treat them."

Two very important ways you can teach your children to be people of integrity are: (1) keep your word to them; and (2) show them that you respect and trust them, and that you do not expect them to lie to you. The first point is obvious; the second, not so clear.

Certainly there are times when you want to check things out to make sure your children are telling the truth—where they're going, who they're with, and so on. But parents who question everything their child says are going to wind up with a problem on their hands. Sooner or later that child will decide, "If that's the way Mom and Dad think I am, then that's the way I'm going to be." That's when the seas of parenting really get rough.

Respect begets respect. Trust begets trust. Integrity begets integrity.

In my opinion the late Wimbledon champion, Arthur Ashe, was one of the finest men ever to play professional tennis. He often talked about what he learned from his parents. One of the most important of these qualities was integrity. Ashe loved to tell this story:

> When I was not quite eighteen years old, I played a tournament in Wheeling, West Virginia...As happened much of the time when I was growing up, I was the only black kid in

the tournament...One night, some of the other kids trashed a cabin; they absolutely destroyed it, and then they decided to say that I was responsible, although I had nothing to do with it. The incident even got into the papers. As much as I denied and protested, those white boys would not change their story.

I rode to Washington from West Virginia with the parents of Dickie Dell, another one of the players. They tried to reassure me, but it was an uncomfortable ride because I was silently worrying about what my father would do and say to me. When I reached Washington, where I was to play in another tournament, I telephoned him in Richmond. As I was aware, he already knew about the incident. When he spoke, he was grim, but he had one question only.

"Arthur Junior, all I want to know is, were you mixed up in that mess?"

"No, Daddy. I wasn't."

He never asked me about it again. He trusted me. With my father, my reputation was solid. I have tried to live so that people would trust my character.

Arthur Ashe not only demonstrated his integrity by being trustworthy, but he also showed it through his trust of others. In the finals of a world championship tennis tournament in 1973, Ashe hit a ball that barely cleared the net on his opponent's side. Stan Smith was playing back, and there seemed to be no way he could get to the ball before it bounced twice. But somehow, racing forward as fast as he could with his racquet stretched out in front of him, he managed to reach the ball in time—and won the point.

Or did he?

The umpire was baffled. The crowd was buzzing, waiting for his decision. Ashe called Smith up to the net and simply asked him, "Stan, did you get to that ball?"

Smith nodded. "I did. I got it."

Ashe conceded the point.

After the match was over—and Ashe had lost—reporters asked him about that pivotal play. Ashe replied, "I wouldn't take just anybody's word for it, but if Stan says he got to the ball, he got to it. I trust his character."

Now, that's integrity.

The old proverb tells us that the apple never falls far from the tree. Of course, there are exceptions to every rule, but it certainly seems to be true that children tend to follow the example their parents set for them. I love the story author Donald Dunn tells about learning integrity from his father, who owned a diesel repair shop.

One day a man walked into the elder Dunn's shop. He said he was driving for a trucking company, and he had a moneymaking idea he wanted to share. His idea was that he would bring in his company's trucks for repairs, and they would add a few unnecessary parts and services to the bill. "We'll let the company pay for it, and you and I will split the difference," the man suggested. "We could make a lot of money."

"Sorry," said Dunn's father. "I can't do that."

"I come through here a lot," the man said, asking Dunn to think it over.

"I don't operate that way."

The truck driver was getting angry. "Everybody does it!" he shouted. "Are you some kind of fool?"

By now Mr. Dunn was completely fed up. He pointed at the door and told the man to leave. But instead of leaving, the truck driver smiled and shook Mr. Dunn's hand. "I own a trucking company," he said. "I've been looking for a mechanic I can trust, and I've finally found one."

Something more was found that day. A son found a role model he could follow for the rest of his life!

**Keep in mind that integrity is pleasing to God.**

*The man of integrity walks securely, but he who takes crooked paths will be found out.*
                                    —Proverbs 10:9

This really ought to be number one on any list of reasons to live in integrity: Because it's important to God. Consider these verses:

*The integrity of the upright guides them, but the unfaithful are destroyed by their duplicity.*
                                    —Proverbs 11:3

*He holds victory in store for the upright, He is a shield to those whose walk is blameless.*
                                    —Proverbs 2:7

*The righteous man leads a blameless life. Blessed are his children after him.*

—Proverbs 20:7

God certainly understands our frailty, but He is pleased when we strive to live a righteous life. David Ireland writes, "Maintaining your integrity is a sure-fire way to know that God is leading you. Be honest about yourself to the Lord. Don't hide or color your actions or thoughts. Integrity will give you peace. There will be a cessation of internal conflict when you decide to walk uprightly before God."

At the same time, there may be an increase of external conflict. One of my favorite Bible stories concerning the high price of integrity can be found in the third chapter of Daniel. It's a story about a king of Babylon named Nebuchadnezzar, and three men of integrity: Shadrach, Meshach, and Abednego. You probably know it. The king—surprise! surprise!—was extremely proud and vain. He had set up a golden statue and ordered everyone in his country to bow down and worship it. Those who refused would be thrown into a blazing furnace.

Everyone went along with the king on this, although most of them probably thought he was wearing his crown a little bit too tight. Shadrach and his friends could have gone along with it too. They could have winked at each other as they bowed down and said, "We don't really believe in this, but—after all—when in Babylon, do as the Babylonians do." Surely God wouldn't be angry with them if He understood that they weren't *really* worshiping the golden statue but were just going through the motions. However, that's not what they did.

> *Shadrach, Meshach, and Abednego replied to the king, "O, Nebuchadnezzar, we do not need to defend ourselves before you in this matter. If we are thrown into the blazing furnace, the God we serve is able to save us from it, and he will rescue us from your hand, O king. But even if he does not, we want you to know, O king, that we will not serve your gods or worship the image of gold you have set up.*
>
> —Daniel 3:16-18

The king was so angry, he had the three men tied up and ordered that the furnace be heated seven times its normal temperature. It was so hot that, when the doors were opened, flames shot out and killed those who were throwing the three condemned men into the fire. What happened next?

> *Then King Nebuchadnezzar leaped to his feet in amazement and asked his advisers, "Weren't there three men that we tied up and threw into the fire?"*
>
> *They replied, "Certainly, O king."*
>
> *He said, "Look! I see four men walking around in the fire, unbound and unharmed, and the fourth looks like a son of the gods."*
>
> —Daniel 3:24-25

The Bible tells us that when those three men came out of the furnace, "the fire had not harmed their bodies, nor was a hair of their heads singed; their robes were not scorched, and there was no smell of fire on them" (Daniel 3:27).

For years, I read that story thinking that Shadrach and his pals knew God was going to deliver them from that furnace. Then one day it occurred to me that they had no such guarantee. They were facing an excruciatingly painful death, but they wouldn't change their behavior to save themselves.

God met them in the fire, and I'm convinced that if you or I get thrown into the fire, He'll meet us there too.

Wow!

God doesn't promise to go before us in every situation, sweeping the obstacles out of the way and giving us a rose-strewn path through life. Jesus went so far as to promise us that anyone who seeks to follow Him will face difficult times in this world. (See John 16:33.) If we strive for absolute integrity in all situations, sooner or later we may find ourselves staring into the mouth of a blazing furnace.

God doesn't promise to spare us from the fiery furnaces of life. But often it is in the furnace that He makes His presence known to us. It's when the flames are threatening to burn us that we come to see how totally dependent we are upon Him. And it's only when we are totally dependent on Him that we see how very much He loves us.

# CHAPTER SIX

# A TINY LITTLE THING
# CALLED WORK

*Genius is 1 percent inspiration*
*and 99 percent perspiration.*
—Thomas Edison

I was on my way to a party for my Orlando Magic colleague Jack Swope—a great guy who was celebrating his twenty-fifth anniversary in the National Basketball Association—and I had the air-conditioner turned up full blast. It was a blazing hot afternoon in mid-August, the time of year when nobody in central Florida wants to be outside. It was about 95 degrees with 100 percent humidity—the kind of day when you start to melt as soon as you leave the comfortable, thermostat-controlled indoors.

As I turned off the main road and into the Isleworth Country Club, I was surprised to see a young man running down the side of the road in my direction. Surely no one would choose to be out running in the hot, thick "soup" of this mid-summer's afternoon. But there he was, his body glistening with perspiration above his black spandex shorts. He wasn't just jogging, either. He was running hard, his arms swinging back and forth as he took long, quick strides. His flat stomach and muscular arms and chest told me that this was no rare occasion. He was obviously accustomed to working out.

"Who in the world would be out running on a day like this?" I thought.

I glanced over as he passed me on the right.

"No, it couldn't be!"

I drove on down the road a hundred yards or so, slowly turned around, and headed back in the runner's direction. As I passed him again, I tried to appear nonchalant, but I took a long, hard look in the rearview mirror. Yes! It was he. No doubt about it.

The man fighting his way through the heat and humidity of a stifling Florida summer afternoon was none other than Tiger Woods! He was wearing dark glasses, but I would have known that face anywhere. After all, I'd just seen him on TV a few days earlier, being interviewed after winning another major PGA tournament.

What was Tiger Woods doing out there on a day like that? Surely he had more comfortable means of getting from one place to another. He could have been riding in the back of an air-conditioned limo, sitting back and sipping an ice-cold lemonade, enjoying the fruits of his victory. Instead, there he was, out in that hot sun, doing what it takes to stay on top—demonstrating the old-fashioned work ethic that made this country great.

On that hot Florida afternoon I remembered something golfer Brad Zwetschke said. Zwetschke, who grew up in the same neighborhood as Tiger Woods, was quoted as saying, "Most of the other kids would play in the pool or be off shooting pool, playing around. Tiger was always practicing...He took the road less traveled while we took the road most traveled."

As I drove on, I watched Tiger in my rearview mirror until he faded into the distance. As I did, I thought of another hard-working athlete, a fellow by the name of Michael Jordan. A few years ago I conducted over fifteen hundred interviews with friends and colleagues of Jordan for my book, *How to Be Like Mike*. One of those I interviewed was then University of Kansas basketball coach Roy Williams. Williams was an assistant coach at North Carolina when Jordan played there and, in fact, helped to recruit him. Roy is now head coach at the University of North Carolina (UNC).

Williams chuckled as he told me of the day, a few years ago, when he and Jordan were paired together in a golf tournament. They got to talking about Tiger Woods, who was in the middle of a record-setting winning streak. Williams asked, "Do you think he's going to be able to keep this up?"

Jordan flashed that famous smile. "Absolutely, Coach," came the reply. "He's just like me." Williams knew right away what Jordan meant. Tiger Woods works hard—very, very hard. He pushes himself to his limit and then some. During the interviews I collected, this point kept coming up over and over again: If you want to be like Mike, you'd better be prepared to work as hard as Mike.

No wonder Michael Jordan was named the Athlete of the Century by ESPN. If you ask me, he was also the Hardest Working Athlete of the twentieth century. Take that kind of talent and combine it with that kind of hard work, and there isn't much of anything you can't do!

By now just about everyone knows the amazing story of Lance Armstrong, who came back from a battle with cancer to become the world's fastest cyclist. Armstrong has been so impressive, in fact, that *Sports Illustrated* named him their Sportsman of the Year for 2002. When they called to tell him about the award, guess where he was? That's right—on his bike—even though it was a cold, blustery day in December. "I gotta suffer a little every day or I'm not happy," he told sportswriter Rick Reilly. Armstrong rides his bike for six hours every day. That's why he's the odds-on favorite to win the Tour De France again this year.

I have known many great winners in my life, and almost all of them had one important thing in common: they worked hard. Like Tiger Woods, Michael Jordan, and Lance Armstrong, they gave everything they had to get to the top; and then, once they were there, they gave everything they had to make sure they stayed there. They weren't looking for shortcuts like steroids and performance-enhancing drugs. They earned their victories.

America's economic system is set up to reward those who work hard—and who run with honesty and integrity toward their goals. Capitalism works when people are getting an honest day's pay for an honest day's work, when consumers are paying an honest price for goods and services, and when businesses are constantly working to improve the products or services they offer.

Our economic system unravels when cheating becomes commonplace, when undercutting the other guy is the order of the day, and when businesses are constantly looking for a way they can improve their profits at the expense of their customers, employees, and the nation at large.

In America today the vast majority of companies still operate the old-fashioned, honest way. Nevertheless, there are others whose prevailing attitude is that profits are king and nothing else matters, and they have pretty much ruined things for the rest of us.

How bad has it gotten? Christian Timbers, one of the nation's top executive-search firms, undertook a study in which it was revealed that nearly one-fourth (23 percent) of all the resumes submitted for top company positions contained exaggerated or misleading information. Another group, Avert Inc., said that 44 percent of all the resumes it double-checked contained at least some lies.

Obviously, far too many people in twenty-first century America are looking for a quick way to get to the top of the mountain. They want fame, power, and fortune, but they are not willing to work for it. Instead, they want to lie and cheat their way to the top. Many are finding out—as their empires topple like so many houses of cards—that there are no shortcuts in life. You can spend your entire life looking for Easy Street, but you'll never find it. People of character work harder. They persevere. They strive for excellence in everything they do.

Here are several reasons why it is important to develop a strong work ethic.

- The Bible commands us to work hard.
- Hard work is the best way to get where you want to go.
- Hard work can bring you personal fulfillment.
- You can prove yourself through hard work.
- Hard work can open the door for inspiration to enter.

### The Bible Commands Us to Work Hard

*Being blessed with a good arm, or God-given talent...*
*Sure, I believe in that quite a bit. But I believe*
*moreso that God gave me the desire to work hard.*
—Roger Clemens

I am convinced that God blesses people who work hard, but I would never say that people are poor because they haven't worked hard. God doesn't call us to judge others. In fact, He warns us not to judge others, saying that He will judge us with the same yardstick we use to measure others. (See Matthew 7:1-2.) It is generally true that hard work is rewarded while laziness brings failure, but there are many exceptions to every rule.

When George W. Bush was running for president, he talked a great deal about "compassionate conservatism." I think a similar term could be applied to the economic system our country has developed over two hundred-plus years: compassionate capitalism. It is a system that rewards those who work hard, but doesn't overlook those who are disadvantaged, disabled, or can't work for some other valid reason. My boss, Rich DeVos, built a tremendous career on compassionate capitalism and even wrote a book about it!

God has always had a special place in His heart for the poor. This can be seen by the fact that He gave the ancient Israelites very specific rules about how they were to harvest their crops. "When you reap the harvest of your land, do not reap to the very edges of your field, or reap the gleanings of your harvest. Do not go over your vineyard a second time or pick up the grapes that have fallen. Leave them for the poor and the alien. I am the Lord your God" (Leviticus 19:9).

I am sure there were people in ancient Israel who tried to take unfair advantage of this system, just as there are people in America today who take advantage of the special provisions our country makes for the disadvantaged. But if an error is going to be made, we need to make it on the side of compassion and generosity.

Having said that, I want to take a brief look at just three of the Bible's many passages that focus on hard work.

The first is 2 Thessalonians 3:10-12, where Paul writes, "For even when we were with you, we gave you this rule: 'If a man will not work, he shall not eat.' We hear that some among you are idle. They are not busy; they are busybodies. Such people we command in the Lord Jesus Christ to settle down and earn the bread they eat."

The second is Ephesians 4:28. "He who has been stealing must steal no longer, but must work, doing something useful with his own hands, that he may have something to share with those in need."

I believe it is necessary to explain why Paul wrote these particular passages. The second chapter of Acts tells us that the early Christians "had everything in common" (Acts 2:44). Luke, the author of Acts, says, "Selling their possessions and goods, they gave to anyone as he had need" (Acts 2:45).

Human nature being what it is, it wasn't long before some unsavory types decided to take advantage of the situation. They knew a good thing when they saw it, and they were more than content to let their hardworking Christian brothers and sisters support them. Paul's words in 2 Thessalonians and Ephesians are meant to remedy this situation—but, again, not to point a finger at those who are truly unable to work.

The third verse I would like us to consider is found in the Sermon on the Mount, where Jesus tells us, "If someone forces you to go one mile, go with him two miles" (Matthew 5:41). What did Jesus mean by this? During Christ's earthly ministry Palestine was under Roman occupation, and the law stipulated that a Roman soldier could ask a citizen in an occupied country to carry his belongings for one mile. If you were a Jew working in your field and a Roman said, "Hey you! I need some help over here," you had to drop whatever you were doing and hop to it. After a mile you were free to go.

I can't imagine that too many Jews joyfully carried the heavy loads of their oppressors. Most of them were probably grumbling under their breath the whole time, wishing there was something they could do to get even. But Jesus said, "Do double what the Roman soldier asks of you. Carry his load for two miles!" Of course, He wasn't talking only about what to do when a Roman soldier ordered you to help him. What Jesus said applies to all areas of life. He was also saying,

"Do more than the boss asks of you."

"Be willing to come in early and work late."

"Work through lunch once in awhile, even if no one asks you to."

"Don't ever be content with doing the bare minimum."

"If someone needs a volunteer for that difficult job, be willing to raise your hand."

Why should we do these things? Not to get credit or to have others notice us and thank us. This is simply what God expects His people to do. I know it's difficult when you work your fingers to the bone and nobody notices, but remember that God notices, and He will make sure that none of your efforts are wasted.

The Bible says that God notices it when you do something as simple as offering a cup of water to a thirsty person, and that someday He will reward you for your kindness. (See Matthew 10:42.) I'm afraid we picture God as a cranky old Ebenezer Scrooge type, always hoping to catch us in some mischief so He can give us a couple of demerits. But my own experience with God tells me that He's much more interested in the good things we do. As strange as it may seem, I am convinced that God wants to be proud of us! And when we work hard to make our corner of the world a better place, I know He is proud of us.

### Hard Work Is the Best Way to Get Where You Want to Go

*If I don't practice for a day, I notice it. If I miss two days, my critics notice it. If I miss three days, the world will know it.*

—Ignacy Paderewski

Coach Jon Gruden led the Tampa Bay Buccaneers to the 2003 Super Bowl. Here's how he did it, in the words of the Bucs' great defensive end, Warren Sapp: "When you're sleeping, he's working. When you're working, he's working. And when you're off? He's still working. That's the way he lives." Again, it takes hard work to get you where you want to go.

Late in his life, artist Pablo Picasso was having dinner with some friends in a small café. Although the other patrons recognized him immediately, most of them kept their distance out of respect for his privacy. But one man strode over to Picasso's table, shoved a napkin in front of him, and said, "Sketch something." When the great artist looked shocked, the man persisted. "Go ahead. I'll pay you for it, of course."

Without saying a word, Picasso took a piece of charcoal out of his pocket and quickly made a crude sketch of a goat. When he had finished, he held it out to the man. "There," he said. "You owe me one hundred thousand dollars."

"One hundred thousand dollars!" the man exclaimed. "Why, it only took you a few seconds to draw that picture."

"Oh no, you're wrong about that," Picasso said, as he crumpled up the napkin and stuck it in his pocket. "It took me forty years." In other words, it was practice and hard work—and plenty of it—that had made Pablo Picasso one of the world's most famous and best-paid artists.

What do you want to be in life? Are you willing to work hard to get there? Are you willing to keep going after you get knocked down once or twice? If somebody tells you that you don't have what it takes to succeed, will you give up, or will you do everything you possibly can to prove them wrong?

As a writer you get used to rejections—sort of. The truth is that rejection always hurts. Some people are simply not going to be interested in whatever you have to say or do. When that happens, you have to have the attitude that you know more about your worth than those who have rejected you.

Over thirty publishers rejected Theodore Geisler, better known as Dr. Seuss, before his first book was finally published and became a runaway bestseller. Jan Karon, whose "Mitford" books have sold hundreds of thousands of copies, did not write her first novel until she was in her fifties. Painter Grandma Moses did not become successful until she was well past retirement age.

Yes! Wherever you want to go, you can get there from here, if you give it all you've got. A woman once rushed up to violinist Fritz Kreisler after an inspiring concert and gushed, "I'd give my life to play as beautifully as you do."

"I did," Kreisler replied.

Many other famous men and women have attributed their success not to genius or talent but hard work.

Genius is the capacity for taking infinite pains.

—Thomas Carlyle

All the genius I may have is merely the fruit of thought and labor.

—Alexander Hamilton

Geniuses themselves don't talk about the gift of genius. They just talk about hard work and long hours.

—J. C. Penney

I have no magic formula. The only way I know to win is through hard work.

—Don Shula

The only thing that separates successful people from those who aren't is the willingness to work very, very hard.

—Helen Gurley Brown

Everything comes to him who hustles while he waits.

—Thomas Edison

If people knew how hard I worked to gain my mastery, it wouldn't seem wonderful at all.

—Michelangelo

I was taught that the way of progress is neither swift nor easy.

—Marie Curie

I wouldn't say that dancing comes so easily to me. I work at it. I practice hour after hour.

—Fred Astaire

Just keep going. Everybody gets better if they just keep at it.

—Ted Williams

I am only an average man, but by George, I work at it harder than the average man!

—Theodore Roosevelt

During World War II several famous dance bands put on a concert in Chicago to raise money for the U. S. war effort. Many of America's most famous musicians were there, including Benny Goodman and a young singer named Frank Sinatra, who was then the featured singer with the Tommy Dorsey Orchestra.

Sinatra remembered later, "I came into this large building where we were rehearsing, and the first person I see is Benny, over in the corner, practicing scales on the clarinet. I had never met him, so I went over and introduced myself." They talked for a while, and then Sinatra asked him why he, one of the greatest clarinetists in the world, would be practicing scales. He figured it was sort of like finding Mozart playing "Chopsticks."

Sinatra said, "Benny looked at me and said, 'If I didn't practice every day, I would only be good. I wouldn't be great.'" Sinatra added, "From then on, I vocalized every day." Sinatra went on to become one of the greatest entertainers of the twentieth century. Would it have happened if he hadn't been inspired by his encounter with Benny Goodman? Perhaps. But then again, perhaps not.

Too many in our society have forgotten that you cannot get where you want to go without working hard to get there. Dreaming about it won't get you there. Neither will cutting corners and looking for shortcuts. Excellence and greatness always have a personal price tag!

### Hard Work Can Bring You Personal Fulfillment

*There's no fun like work.*
—Thomas Lipton
Founder, Lipton Tea

Some Christians are confused about the nature of work. They read the first few chapters of Genesis and conclude that work is one of the curses that fell upon humankind when we fell from grace. They especially point to Genesis 3:17-19, where God tells Adam, "Cursed is the ground because of you; through painful toil you will eat of it all the days of your life. It will produce thorns and thistles for you, and you will eat the plants of the field. By the sweat of your brow you will eat your food until you return to the ground, since from it you were taken."

When I read these verses, it seems apparent to me that the *curse* brought thorns and thistles into the world—*not* hard work. Anyone who has ever tried to put in a new lawn knows how awful this curse can be. In Florida we have a terrible plant called "sand spurs." It looks like grass when it first comes up, and it will take over your yard in no time if you let it. Before you know it, it produces thousands of stickers, covered with tiny, needle-sharp points.

Every time I see a small patch of sandspurs, I am reminded that this world is not what God originally meant it to be. I imagine that in the world before the fall, thornless roses sprang up all over the place without being planted. The grass was lush and green, and there was no such thing as a dandelion or a stinkweed. Now, because of sin, it's the bad stuff like weeds that grows naturally, while good things like flowers, fruit trees, and vegetables won't grow without plenty of attention and hard work.

Work has always been part of God's plan for man. I know this because the second chapter of Genesis says that soon after the first man was created, "The Lord God took the man and put him in the Garden of Eden to work it and take care of it" (Geneses 2:15).

After Moses led the Israelites out of Egypt, they wandered in the wilderness for more than forty years. During that time God provided food and water, and made it so that their clothes and shoes never wore out. In many ways the Israelites were living in a welfare state, with all their needs taken care of. Yet all the while they were dreaming about the land God had told them about—the promised land which flowed with milk and honey. However, when they finally reached the promised land, God stopped dropping food from Heaven, milk came by milking cows, honey had to be gathered, and the cows and bees needed care.

I feel certain we will find jobs waiting for us when we get to heaven. If so, we can be certain that the tasks God has planned for us will suit us perfectly. We will find satisfaction and fulfillment in doing what God created us to do. Meanwhile, it is possible to find a little piece of heaven here on earth by doing something that is suited to our talents, abilities, and personalities—and doing it with all our might.

I believe that one of the reasons our society has fallen into scandal is that too many people forgot that work can be its own reward. It can be the means through which we obtain self-satisfaction and fulfillment. It can help us develop our talents and skills and thus improve ourselves. Most importantly, it can be something that makes the world a better place.

Work should never be something you do just to make money or to pass the time. If you hate your job and are just counting the days to retirement, then you're not doing what you should be doing. Only when you find something that you love to do and then do it with all the energy God gave you will your work become the rich, rewarding profession God intended it to be.

Writer Mamie McCullough says, "We often feel hard work is a curse to be endured. Nothing could be further from reality! The truth is, work is a blessing." She goes on, "Work is often an antidote for whatever ails us. It is one of the best medicines for the multitude of maladies that attack mankind. Know that hard work is a precious gift that enhances your well being. Be thankful if you have useful work to do. It is a blessing above all others."

That reminds me of a story about Thomas Edison, who was known for spending one hundred hours or more in his laboratory each week. Once, after a particularly long, hard day, Edison came home to a sympathetic wife who told him he'd been working too hard. "You need to take a vacation," she told him.

"But where on earth would I go?" he asked.

"Just decide where you would rather be than anyplace else on earth," she told him.

The great inventor nodded, "Very well. I'll go there tomorrow."

The next morning he got up and went back to his laboratory.

I love what the late bandleader Lawrence Welk said. "To be granted some kind of useable talent, and to be able to use it to the fullest extent of which you are capable—this, to me, is a kind of joy that is almost un-equalled. I have found it in music; my father in farm-ing. I know others who have found it in practicing medicine or running a bakery or driving a truck—in running a bakery that makes the best kind of bread or in driving a truck better than anyone else. That's the kind of achievement that makes a man happy."

I can think of few things sadder than putting in eight or nine hours a day doing something you really don't want to do. What a waste of the time and talent God has given you! If you find that you spend your en-tire workweek looking forward to Friday, then you owe it to yourself to look for something else to do with your life. An old Bantu proverb says, "Work is good, provided you do not forget to live." I would add, "Work is good, provided you are able to find life in your work." Believe me, it is possible to enjoy all the days of the week, including Monday. I know from per-sonal experience.

Author Bobb Biehl finds more enjoyment and ful-fillment in his work than most people I know. He lists six ways you can know for certain that you're doing what God wants you to do:

- **It will involve your greatest single strength.**

- **You will love it**—so much that you'd be willing to do it, even if you didn't get paid for doing it.

- **You will never tire of it.** Yes, you may get fatigued from time to time, but overall you will enjoy what you are doing and the results it brings.

- **Others will affirm you in what you are doing.** Your decision to go into a certain field will be affirmed by your closest friends, who will say things like, "I think you've found your niche."

- **You will earn an adequate income.** In order for anything to qualify as your life's work, it must pay you enough to make a living by doing it. Otherwise, even though it may be a very important part of your life, it is just a hobby.

- **It will represent a significant use of the rest of your life.** In other words, it will bring you personal fulfillment. Regarding this point, Bobb says, "The lack of fulfillment is the reason $500,000-per-year corporate executives resign from corporate America to teach college for $40,000."

Harvey Firestone said, "The man or woman who doesn't accomplish anything doesn't get much out of life. I believe most men will make good if they find the work they are happy doing."

## You Can Prove Yourself Through Hard Work

*The world is full of willing people. Some willing*
*to work, the rest willing to let them.*

—Robert Frost

I've never viewed myself as an extraordinarily talented person. School never came easy to me, and I wasn't what you'd call a star on the baseball diamond, even though I played four years in college and spent a couple of years in the pros. Whatever I accomplished was achieved through hard work, and plenty of it!

I suppose you could say that I am a classic overachiever. I have an incessant inner drive that pushes me on. The only way I know how to succeed is to outwork other people. And do you know what? It works well. I recommend it!

Last January I ran in the 2003 Disney Marathon—my twenty-sixth marathon. Believe me, they don't get any easier. Long before I reached the midway mark, my body was screaming, "Stop! Take a break!" On this occasion race organizers had put up several signs along the way, each bearing an encouraging quote. At the 10-mile mark stood a sign with this quote from hockey great, Bobby Clarke: "If you push the human body, it will respond." At the 13-mile marker another sign said, "The harder you work, the harder it is to surrender."

Eighteen miles in, another sign reminded all the runners, "Running is the greatest metaphor for life because you get out of it what you put into it." There were two more quotes posted near the end of the event to keep us encouraged down the home stretch. The first was a quote from Olympic gold medallist Sohn Kee-Chung, "The human body can do so much, then the heart and spirit must take over." Finally, from the late Steve Prefontaine, "A lot of people race to see who's the fastest. I race to see who has the most guts."

Those signs helped me muster the strength and courage I needed to keep putting one foot in front of the other. They reminded me of the joys that came from doing your best in every endeavor. Sadly, many people in this world work just hard enough to get by. They hang on to their jobs because there's no real reason to fire them, but there's no reason to promote them either. Such are many of the people you will pass on your way up the ladder, if you're willing to work hard.

Author/motivational speaker Zig Ziglar says: "We need to teach our children that, for eight hours a day, competition is extremely tough; but when we work one more hour, 90 percent of the competition will drop out. At that point, we have an open door to greater productivity and a promotion.

"When we accept additional responsibilities we become, in essence, like sailing vessels. On a sailing vessel, the more sail that is hoisted, the faster and farther it will go. In life, if we want to go farther and faster, we must hoist more sail or put more of ourselves into a project."

In a recent poll undertaken by *USA Today*, 71 percent of those surveyed agreed that hard work helps a person get further in life. Korn/Ferry Vice-President Virgil Baldi says, "The successful people that I see in our business are people that are really driven—people that get a kick out of what they're doing." David Peasback, president of executive recruiting firm Heidrich & Struggles, reflected on what makes people successful, "I don't think you can get away from the fact that it's long hours."

Recently I came upon another remarkable piece of research done by Dr. Benjamin Bloom, professor of education at the University of Chicago and Northwestern University. His five-year study showed that drive and dedication are far more important than talent when it comes to winning top honors. He found that very few of those who are now at the top of their chosen professions demonstrated exceptional natural talent or ability for what they do.

More than 95 percent of those chosen for Dr. Bloom's study—Olympic athletes to concert pianists to neurosurgeons—chose their careers because of encouragement from their families. Dr. Bloom says that when he began the survey, he expected to find that all of these top achievers had been channeled into their current professions because someone had recognized great talent in them early in life.

"But we found just the reverse," he says. "These people took lessons in their fields because this was what their families encouraged and liked." In other words, all of these people reached the top of their professions in the same way—plenty of practice and hard work. Excellence never comes cheaply. It involves desire, discipline, and determination.

Renowned baritone Sherrill Milnes is a good example of someone who put in long, hard hours in an attempt to become better at his chosen profession. His wife, Nancy Stokes Milnes, told the *New York Opera Newsletter* that when she and her husband had dinner with a famous voice coach, they played him a recording Sherill had made when he was in college. Then they asked him, "What do you think about this voice?"

The voice coach shook his head sadly, "Not a chance," he said. "Don't encourage this person. Tell him to get a day job."

When Sherill said, "Why, that's me," the voice coach's jaw dropped. "I'll never discourage another singer again," he said.

Mrs. Milnes writes, "You never can tell. The most gifted person can walk into your studio and achieve very little. Someone whose talent seems okay can work and work until he or she can make it. You can't tell people what their dreams are, or what the limits of their dreams should be. It's up to them to tell you."

James E. Byrnes, who served as secretary of state under Harry Truman, once said that he learned early in life that the difference between those who succeed in life and those who don't is determined by three little words, "and then some." He explained, "The top people did what was expected of them, and then some. They were considerate and thoughtful of others, and then some. They met their obligations and responsibilities fairly and squarely, and then some. They were good friends to their friends, and then some. They could be counted on in an emergency, and then some."

These are excellent words to live by—and then some.

### Hard Work Can Open the Door for Inspiration to Enter

*The great composer does not set to work because*
*he is inspired but becomes inspired because*
*he is working. Beethoven, Wagner, Mozart, and Bach*
*all settled down, day-after-day, to the job at hand.*
*They didn't waste time waiting for inspiration.*

—Ernest Newman, Author

I knew a woman who wanted to write a book. When she first told me about it, she was very excited. She felt that God had inspired her to write a fictional account, which expanded on the life of a biblical character. Every so often after that, when our paths crossed, I'd ask her how the book was coming. The first few times I saw her, she told me she was researching the subject. She had discovered numerous interesting tidbits about this character and the times in which she had lived. This was certainly going to be a well-researched novel, and I was looking forward to reading it.

Months went by and my friend was still researching her topic. I asked her when she was going to start writing. That's when she confessed that she was having some trouble getting started. She was "waiting for inspiration."

I told her what I've heard from many writers. Getting started on the actual writing is the hardest thing to do. I also told her that the only way to get started is to sit down at the word processor and start typing. What you write may sound terrible, but at least you're putting something on paper—or screen—and you can always go back over it later and make it better.

She nodded but didn't do anything about it. The next time I saw her, she acted as if she didn't want to talk to me. I knew it couldn't be because of my breath, dandruff, or my personality—so I figured it must have to do with the book. I'm pretty good at picking up clues, so I never asked her about it again. And she never brought it up again. Too bad. I think it would have been a good book, and it might have touched thousands of hearts with God's love. But it will never see the light of day. I wish my friend had paid attention to this advice from speaker Joe Sabah: "You don't have to be great to start, but you do have to start to be great."

I realize that there are rare occasions when inspiration comes out of the blue. Paul McCartney says he woke up one morning with the tune of *Yesterday* running through his mind. Before claiming it as his own, he even asked several other people if they had heard the tune before. They hadn't, so McCartney wrote it down on paper, and it became the most-recorded song of all times.

Something like that is a rare exception to the rule. I believe inspiration comes mostly through work. For example, occasionally I will be working on a book, and the manuscript will begin to go off in an entirely different direction than I had intended. What's happened is that I have become inspired about something important I needed to say. Inspiration did not come because I was waiting for it but because I was already working. As Thomas Edison said, "Everything comes to him who hustles while he waits."

It is reported that when someone asked Alexander the Great how he was able to conquer the world, he replied, "By not delaying." Opera great, Beverly Sills, said, "You may be disappointed if you fail, but you are doomed if you don't try."

A few years ago Ruth and I went to see Kenny Rogers in concert, and we had an opportunity to chat with him before the show. Rogers has been entertaining most of his life, starting out in the early 1960s with the New Christy Minstrels. I asked him how he managed to keep himself motivated night after night, even when he didn't feel like it. He smiled and said, "When I hear the music and step on the stage and see the people, it gets me going, even if my spirits are down or my voice is tired. The enthusiasm returns when the music starts. The people have paid a lot of money and traveled to see me, so I feel I owe them my best effort, even if I don't feel 100 percent."

Do you want to change your world? If so, you have to put yourself in a position where God can work through you—where He can inspire you to greatness!

# CHAPTER SEVEN

# STRIVE FOR A
# MATURE ATTITUDE

*Emotional maturity is a preface for a sense of values.*
—Vince Lombardi

When you were a child, did your mother ever tell you to act your age? Mine did. At the time it hurt my feelings, but now that I'm an adult, I know how important it is to behave in a mature, sensible way. A mature person is able to wait their turn. They understand that they are not going to get everything they want out of life. They are able to delay gratification.

The mature businessperson or entrepreneur understands that it takes time to build a profitable company, and that you can't expect to start turning multi-million dollar profits overnight. They take the long-range view of things, preferring long-term stability and growth over being a flash-in-the-pan that is here today and gone tomorrow.

My good friend, speaker-author Jay Strack, works with thousands of young people every year. He says that a person reaches maturity "when the little girl or little boy decides to sit down permanently, and the young woman or young man decides to stand up permanently."

In her book, *The Best of Dear Abby*, the late advice columnist Abigail Van Buren says that a class of sixth graders from Milwaukee asked for her definition of *maturity*. She says, "I hurriedly dashed off a succinct and over-simplified reply. It was published in their school newspaper and a copy sent to me. It looked so good in print, I decided to use it in my column."

> Maturity is the ability to do a job whether you're supervised or not; to finish a job once it's started; to carry money without spending it; and to bear injustice without wanting to get even.

That's a pretty good place to start. What Dear Abby is saying here—and I agree with her 100 percent—is that the mark of a truly mature person is the ability to exercise *self-discipline* in every area of life. The best way to learn self-discipline is through developing *good habits*. A person who has good habits is consistent in every area of their life, and consistency ultimately brings success

I have interviewed dozens of leaders in various careers—such as business, athletics, government, entertainment, and education—and the vast majority of them credit their success to consistency. They do not see themselves as incredibly brilliant or as inherently better than other people. Most consider themselves to be average people who have worked consistently and with great effort to reach their goals.

In sports we talk about concentrating on the fundamentals. If you do the little things well consistently, you will probably win a majority of your games. For a near-perfect example, watch Tiger Woods the next time a major golf tournament is on television. He is a model of consistency on every hole. Watch the way he hits the ball off the tee. Observe how he follows through. See the way he takes the time to line up a putt. He never gets flustered or distracted. He stays focused on what he is doing at all times and, as a result, does almost everything right.

The late Ted Williams is another good example. Williams was the last Major League baseball player to hit over .400 in a season. That means he had more than four base hits in every ten trips to the batter's box. Williams knew the strike zone and rarely swung at balls that weren't in it. Thus, throughout his career he was a consistent *frustration* to opposing pitchers and hit his way into the Hall of Fame.

Wayne Gretzky, who is known to every hockey fan as "The Great One," once explained that his tremendous career was built on a foundation of good habits. "No matter who you are, no matter how good an athlete you are," he said, "we are creatures of habit. The better your habits are, the better they'll be in pressure situations."

What habits do you need to develop?

The best definition of maturity I know is found in the fifth chapter of Galatians, where the apostle Paul lists nine character traits that he calls the fruit of the Spirit. They are love, joy, peace, patience, kindness, goodness, faithfulness, gentleness, and self-control.

### Love

*This is the message you have heard*
*from the beginning: We should love one another.*
—1 John 3:11

Some people would be quick to tell you that love has no place in the business world. Unless, of course, we're talking about the love of money. The Bible, however, tells us in 1 Timothy 6:10 that the love of money is the root of all kinds of evil. What do you suppose is in the hearts of executives who fill their pockets with gold at the expense of their employees and customers? It's certainly not love.

The Bible describes love in 1 Corinthians 13:4-7. "Love is patient, love is kind. It does not envy, it does not boast, it is not proud. It is not rude, it is not self-seeking, it is not easily angered, it keeps no record of wrong. Love does not delight in evil but rejoices with the truth. It always protects, always trusts, always hopes, always perseveres."

I urge you to take a minute right now and ask yourself this important question: Who do I love? I'm sure you love your parents, your children, your spouse, your brothers and sisters, and your friends. Hopefully, loving those people comes naturally. But God expects us to demonstrate a much wider and broader circle of love. We are called to love *everyone*.

Ask yourself honestly if you love your neighbors—even the ones with the annoying dog that barks all night long. Do you love your co-workers—even the ones who loaf around and leave you to do most of the work? Do you love your bosses? Your teachers? Do you love the people you come into contact with in other parts of your life—the cashiers, the clerks, the waiters and waitresses?

It has been said that love is a choice, and it takes a mature person to make that choice. The apostle John hits a nerve when he says, "Whoever does not know love does not know God, because God is love" (1 John 4:8). And, "For anyone who does not love his brother, whom he has seen, cannot love God, whom he has not seen" (1 John 4:20).

Jesus even takes things a step further: "You have heard that it was said, 'Love your neighbor and hate your enemy.' But I tell you: Love your enemies and pray for those who persecute you" (Matthew 5:43-44).

Do you love the guy who cuts you off in rush-hour traffic and then gestures at you as if you were at fault?

Do you love the telemarketer who calls during your dinner?

Do you love the bureaucrat who's rude to you after you've stood in line for an hour and a half to renew your driver's license?

The truly mature person does not go around with a chip on their shoulder, ready to fight at the slightest provocation. They demonstrate a loving, caring attitude in everything they do and help to make the world a better place. That's why the first habit we should strive to develop is an attitude of love.

## Joy

*The hardest habit of all to break*
*is the terrible habit of happiness.*
—Theodosia Garrison

Joy doesn't come from having more money than anyone else. It isn't the feeling you get when you receive the promotion that your co-worker really wanted. It doesn't spring out of an absence of troubles in your life, but rather from an understanding that God is using whatever troubles you experience to strengthen your character and make you a better human being.

Joy is an inner sense of peace, contentment, and happiness that stays with you even when things aren't going your way. Joy is keeping a smile on your face when people look at you and ask, "What in the world have they got to be smiling about?"

For the most part, joy comes from God's presence in your life. It's impossible not to have joy if you're walking with God on a daily basis. But joy also comes from maintaining an attitude of gratitude, from doing what the old song says:

*Count your many blessings,*
*name them one by one.*
*And it will surprise you*
*what the Lord has done.*

Rick Warren writes, "When you grasp the eternal consequences of your character development, you'll pray fewer 'Comfort me' prayers ('Help me to feel good') and more 'Conform me' prayers ('Use this to make me more like you'). You know you are maturing when you begin to see the hand of God in the random, baffling, and seemingly pointless circumstances of life."

During my career in sports I've had the privilege of knowing many men and women who seemed to have joy in their hearts at all times—but two in particular stand out in my mind. The first is Ernie Banks, who did an outstanding job of playing shortstop for some horrible Chicago Cubs' teams during the 1950s and 1960s.

Most players with Banks' talent would have demanded a trade to a better team, but Banks never did. He kept going out there day after day, season after season, with a smile on his face and an encouraging word on his lips for everyone he spoke to. I'm sure Ernie Banks had bad days. There must have been times when he snapped at reporters or yelled at one of his teammates for making a bonehead play. But I never saw that side of him. All I ever saw was a man who enjoyed the game of baseball so much that he always said, "Let's play two," even when it was early April and bitterly cold at Wrigley Field. What a joy he was.

The second person who comes to mind is Ervin "Magic" Johnson. He was one tough customer on the basketball court. I can't tell you how many times he broke my heart with a last-second shot or a steal in a crucial situation. But no matter how many times he beat us, I couldn't help but love him because of his joyful, exuberant attitude, which showed in the huge smile he always wore. Yes, Magic Johnson made some serious mistakes in other areas of his personal life, and he is living with the consequences, but when it came to having a joyful attitude that lifted his teammates and helped them play at their peak level, there was nobody better.

How do you choose joy in a world that is confronted by terrorism, violence, and suffering on a daily basis? The only way I know is simply to remind yourself several times a day that God is still in charge of everything in the universe—including your own life. Even when life seems like a trip through a minefield, you can rest in the knowledge that Jesus, the Good Shepherd, knows where every single one of those mines is buried. You can trust Him to lead you safely, even through "the valley of the shadow of death."

Just as I was writing this paragraph, about 9 p.m., I was interrupted by a telephone call from my son, David. (This book is dedicated to David and his wife Shawvana.) David is a U.S. Marine and was calling from Camp Pendleton, California. He said, "Dad, I don't have much time to talk. Our unit is leaving for Kuwait in a few hours. I just wanted to call and tell you." He went on to assure me, "I'm not afraid. I'm excited. It's almost like I've been practicing for a ball game, and now we get a chance to play."

I said, "David, let's pray," and we did. Then I told him, "Never forget that the Lord is with you and will lead you. Keep your eyes on Him."

Before he hung up, he said, "I'm going to get Saddam for you, Dad."

Of course, it makes me uneasy to think of David going into combat. It also makes me uneasy to think that his unit will be landing on an aircraft carrier. But I know that David's life is in God's hands, and that eases my anxiety, comforts me, and brings joy to my heart. We can also maintain a joyful attitude by remembering the Bible promise that, "Our present sufferings are not worth comparing with the glory that will be revealed in us" (Romans 8:18). When things look bleak, remember that God has a happy ending planned for all of this.

### Peace

*From the time you get up in the morning*
*to the time you go to sleep at night, your habits*
*largely control the words you say, the things you do,*
*and the ways you react and respond.*
—Brian Tracy, Author

I've had people say to me, "I'm just a hot-headed guy. I have a quick temper. There's nothing I can do about it." My reaction is always the same: "Yes, there is something you can do about it. You can learn to control your temper, even in the most stressful and difficult situations."

The last thing a basketball team needs is a guy who's going to get angry in a critical situation. You don't want a player who's going to get a technical foul by throwing the basketball into the stands, swearing at the referee, or getting into a shoving match with an opposing player. I've seen so many games turn on a situation like that. It doesn't really matter how much talent a player has. If he's a hotheaded troublemaker, no one's going to want him on their team. This holds true in sports, business, and other areas of life.

If you're naturally a quick-tempered person, that may not be what you want to hear, but the good news is that you really can change the way you act. Like everything else we are discussing in this chapter, peace comes primarily through knowing God and experiencing His daily presence in our lives. But it's also true—again, like everything else we are discussing in this chapter—that having a peaceful frame of mind can be a habit. Author Brian Tracy says, "You can learn any habit that you consider desirable or necessary if you work at it long enough and hard enough."

That doesn't mean it's easy to learn a new habit. You may have to work terribly hard at it. I've heard it said that you have to do something nineteen times before it becomes a habit. I have no idea where they came up with nineteen times, and I think it's more than that for me. I also know that it is much easier to learn a good new habit than it is to "unlearn" an old, bad one.

As someone has said, "A bad habit is like a soft, warm bed. Easy to get into, but not so easy to get out of."

Once you have acquired a habit, it takes on a life of its own. It becomes second nature to you. So practice having a peaceful attitude. Learn to breathe deeply and relax. Listen to quiet music or relaxation tapes if you need to. Remind yourself often that you are determined to demonstrate an attitude of peace in all situations. *You can do it.* Promise yourself that you will not let other people or difficult situations make you angry or ill at ease. Resolve to remain cool, calm, and collected because it will be good for you physically, emotionally, and spiritually. Plus, it will keep you from making angry mistakes that can really foul things up for you.

Motivational speaker and author Zig Ziglar says, "Fear is a habit. So are self-pity, defeat, anxiety, despair, and hopelessness." He goes on to say, "You can eliminate these bad habits with two simple resolutions. (Now, I did not say it would be easy...I said it would be simple.) The resolutions are: 'I can,' and 'I will.' Make these two resolutions and you will become an even bigger winner in the game of life."

In his classic book, *The Greatest Salesman in the World*, Og Mandino said, "In truth, the only difference between those who have failed and those who have succeeded lies in the difference of their habits. Good habits are the key to all success. Bad habits are the unlocked door to failure; thus, the first law I will obey, which precedes all others, is..."I will form good habits and become their slave.'"

I also like what Frank B. Gilbreth says. "We're worn into grooves by time...by our habits...By choosing our habits, we determine the grooves into which time will wear us, and these are the grooves that enrich our lives and make for ease of mind, peace, happiness... achievement."

## Patience

*Managers must have the discipline not to keep pulling up the flowers to see if the roots are healthy.*
—Robert Townsend
President of Avis Rent-a-Car

A mature person is able to delay gratification. They don't throw a temper tantrum if they don't get everything they want right now.

On my way to work the other day, I saw a car with a bumper sticker that said, "I want the world, and I want it now!" I'm sure the driver was trying to be funny, at least I hope he was, but I know some people who really feel that way. Some of them are—or were— top officers in American corporations (which is another reason we find ourselves in such a mess).

Patient people are able to pass up doing something that might be fun right now to concentrate on the bigger picture. When they run into problems on the job or in their marriages, they are willing to do whatever is necessary to work things out. They don't change jobs, relationships, or spouses the moment the going gets tough. They are able to stick with the task at hand until it is finished.

Moses demonstrated a mature attitude when, "He chose to be mistreated along with the people of God rather than to enjoy the pleasures of sin for a short time" (Hebrews 11:25). He patiently chose lasting value over temporary enjoyment.

Part of the problem for us inhabitants of the twenty-first century is that we've become accustomed to having everything "right now." We cook with microwaves. We communicate via e-mail. We can access enormous volumes of information instantaneously through the Internet. When a major news event happens half the world a way, CNN takes us there. We are moving ahead so fast that a personal computer is outdated almost as soon as you buy it. The strange thing is, the faster we go, the less patience we seem to have. Here's a perfect motto for the modern American: "Faster! Faster! Faster!"

For an example of what I'm talking about, just follow the stock market for a couple of weeks. I can't remember another time when the Dow swung back and forth like a roller coaster on an almost daily basis. We get some bad economic news, everyone rushes to sell, and the Dow falls by 150 points. The next day we get a glimmer of hope, everyone buys, and we're up by 150. Too many investors are impatient. They want to make a fortune in the market and they want to do it right now. They've forgotten that slow and steady really does win the race.

I recently read about a fascinating survey conducted by the National Sales Executive Association. Here's what they found:

- 80 percent of all new sales are made after the fifth call to the same prospect.

- 48 percent of all salespersons make one call. Then, if they don't make a sale, they remove that prospect from their list.

- Another 25 percent give up after being turned down twice.

- An additional 12 percent quit after three calls.

- Only 10 percent continue to call—and these are the ones who make 80 percent of the sales.

Patience pays off!

### Kindness

*You can't claim to be kind unless you are habitually kind...you show kindness without even thinking about it.*
—Rick Warren

A mature person understands that it's okay to be kind. They don't go around with a brash, tough-guy attitude, pushing people out of their way and demanding, "You looking at me?"

When are we finally going to figure out that the very best way to help ourselves is to help other people? Jesus wasn't kidding around when He said that we get back what we give, that we reap what we sow, and that we will be treated the same way we treat others.

Kindness is one of the greatest ways to preach the Gospel without saying a word. Kindness draws people to you. Besides, the person who is always kind to others shows that he has faith in God's ability to make things turn out as they should. On the other hand, a man or woman who thinks they have to be tough to make it in this world is demonstrating a lack of faith. That kind of thinking is in line with Darwin's "survival of the fittest." It doesn't square with the Bible's admonition to clothe ourselves with kindness. (See Colossians 3:12.)

Although I don't always succeed, my intention is to do something especially kind every day. I give a compliment or a word of encouragement when I can. When I'm eating out, I tell the servers that I appreciate the good service they give me. When I hear something good about someone, I share it with that person. In rush-hour traffic I'll slow down so the guy next to me can change lanes and not miss his exit. These are little things, but a little thing can make a big difference in someone's life.

As I look back over my life, I remember several occasions when others were especially kind to me. In June of 1962, when I was a senior at Wake Forest University, our baseball team fell one game short of an appearance at the College World Series. My father drove all the way from my hometown of Wilmington, Delaware, to Gastonia, North Carolina, to watch us play a crucial game against Florida State. A win would send us to Omaha.

A loss would mean the end of our season. As it turned out, we lost a heartbreaker to the Seminoles in eleven innings.

I didn't know at the time, but that loss was only the beginning of my heartbreak. My father, whom I loved and admired, died in a car crash on his way home. The day of my dad's funeral, I was surprised to see my college baseball coach, Jack Stallings, at the church. He had driven all the way from North Carolina to show me his support and love. I have never forgotten his kind, gracious act. He brightened one of the worst days of my life.

I've also had some encounters with people who were flat-out mean for no reason at all. Some of those confrontations still sting twenty or thirty years later. At the All-Star game in Cleveland a few years ago, the NBA celebrated its fiftieth anniversary by honoring its Fifty Greatest Players of All Time, and a beautiful coffee-table book was prepared for the occasion. Everyone was going around with their books, getting them signed.

On three separate occasions I approached Kareem Abdul Jabbar and asked him to autograph my book, and each time he turned me down flat, even though I've known him for years. It was not a good feeling, and it made me wonder how he'd react to a complete stranger who wanted an autograph.

Two years later Kareem was the featured speaker at a luncheon I was emceeing in Tampa. Now, I've told you that I believe in being persistent. I took my book, and once again asked him to sign it. This time he smiled and asked, "You mean the one I didn't sign in Cleveland?" Then he proceeded to sign it.

Jabbar gave a wonderful speech that day and received a standing ovation. Afterwards, when I went up to tell him what a great job he'd done, I saw tears in his eyes. Today I have nothing but respect for the man. Even so, I can still feel the sting of the day he refused to sign my book.

I have similar feelings about an encounter with Warren Sapp, the great defensive end of the Tampa Bay Buccaneers. A few years ago I played in Major League Baseball's alumni game at Al Lang Field in St. Petersburg. What a wonderful treat it was for me to be a big leaguer for one night! Sapp was one of my teammates on that occasion, and we had a great time talking about basketball, which is one of Sapp's passions.

A few months later I was in Tampa for a meeting and stopped for lunch at a Sweet Tomato Restaurant, which features an all-you-can-eat buffet. As I went to my table, I saw Warren Sapp sitting at a table with some of his teammates. (Those guys had so much food stacked up in front of them that I'm sure the Sweet Tomato didn't make any money that day.) I naturally thought I'd go over and say hello.

"Warren," I said. "How are..."

Before I could finish, he threw up his hands and barked, "Don't come near me, man!" Shocked, I stopped in my tracks, and he ordered. "Don't come one step closer."

As I slinked back to my table, I thought, "Man, oh, man! Does it really cost that much to be nice?"

I don't know what was going on that day, but frankly, it changed my entire perspective on the Tampa Bay Buccaneers.

How do you want people to remember the encounters they've had with you? Our small efforts at kindness can change people's lives more than we will ever know. Since it takes so little time and energy to change the world for the better, why not make an effort to do it every day?

## Goodness

*Those who say it's easy to be good*
*have never tried to be good.*
—C. S. Lewis

Most of us know instinctively what it means to be good. Being good makes us feel good inside because we know we're pleasing to God. If we're not good, we feel crummy because we know we haven't acted the way God wants us to act. As we've discussed previously, only those who have seared their consciences through continually bad behavior don't feel a twinge of guilt when they misbehave.

The Bible has a great deal to say about being good. In Luke 6:27, Jesus commands us to "do good to those who hate you." The apostle Paul writes, "Let us not grow weary in doing good, for at the proper time we will reap a harvest if we do not give up. Therefore, as we have opportunity, let us do good to all people" (Galatians 6:9-10). He also writes, "For we are God's workmanship, created in Christ Jesus to do good works, which God prepared in advance for us to do" (Ephesians 2:10).

The prophet Micah says, "He has showed you, O man, what is good. And what does the Lord require of you? To act justly and to love mercy and to walk humbly with your God" (Micah 6:8).

Be good. You just might change the world!

### Faithfulness

*A husband who is faithful to his wife*
*most of the time is not faithful to her at all...There is*
*only one way to develop the habits of Christlike*
*character, and that is to practice them all the time.*

—Rick Warren

It is no accident that Jesus taught us to pray that we would not be led into temptation. The very best way to remain faithful is to completely avoid those things that would tempt you to be unfaithful. If you're tempted to drink, don't go to parties where alcohol is served. If you're tempted to pornography, then you shouldn't have cable television that brings it right into your house. If gambling is a problem for you, then you shouldn't be planning a vacation to Las Vegas!

Confederate General Stonewall Jackson was a proud and ambitious man, but he was also a Christian, an elder in the Presbyterian Church who felt that his desire for fame was at odds with what God wanted for him. At the high-point of his fame, Jackson quit reading newspapers because he didn't want to read things about himself that would make him prideful.

The men who served with Jackson also noticed that he never drank whisky with them. When asked why, he replied, "Because I like the taste of it, and when I discovered that to be the case, I made up my mind to do without it altogether." He was determined to be faithful in all things.

What things should you and I avoid? I believe there are eight specific temptations satan uses to trip us up and cause us to be unfaithful.

### Alcohol

The television commercials make alcohol look so cool! All those healthy, happy, beautiful young people guzzling down beer and having the time of their lives! I have two things to say about that: First, satan does a good job of making all his temptations look good. Second, you can't expect a brewing company to develop a TV commercial that shows a wino staggering through skid row with a bottle in his hand. Nor can you expect them to show film footage of the carnage caused by drunk drivers every year—American highways littered with scraps of twisted metal, glass and dead bodies—entire families' dreams destroyed forever. More than half of all fatal auto accidents in the United States involve alcohol.

The truth is that alcohol does not make you "cool." It impairs your judgment, slurs your speech, slows your reflexes, and can cause you to act like a complete fool. Nobody is saying that you will wind up a hopeless wino just because you take a drink or two. But that wino didn't start out with the ambition of wearing the same clothes for a week, sleeping in doorways, and spending his days staggering around in a drunken stupor. It all started with a single drink. Since that's what drinking can do to you, why take a chance?

**Drugs**

In Deuteronomy 18:10, God says, "Let no one be found among you...who practices divination or sorcery." The root word translated into English as "sorcery," is also root of the English word, "pharmaceuticals;" in other words, drugs or narcotics. I've seen tremendous damage and heartache caused by drugs, so the very best advice I can give is to stay away!

**Tobacco**

I had a friend who wanted to overcome years of alcoholism, so he checked himself into a treatment center. As far as I know, he never took another drink. After that he decided to give up smoking. He tried everything he could think of, including hypnosis, anti-smoking aids, and another treatment center or two. Nothing worked. In desperation he told me, "Giving up alcohol was nothing compared to trying to give up cigarettes." This story does not have a happy ending. My friend could not quit smoking and died of lung cancer in his early sixties. Tobacco is not only dangerously addictive; it's deadly, killing over one million people every year.

I am currently working on a book about Walt Disney called *How to Be Like Walt*. My research for this book, including interviews with Disney's family and friends, has led me to feel as if I knew Walt Disney personally. I have come to appreciate his genius even more than I ever did before. There was one thing Walt Disney did wrong, however. He chain-smoked cigarettes. He died from lung cancer at sixty-five, depriving the world of many more years of his great talent.

More recently, one of my favorite writers, Stephen Ambrose, died of cancer linked to smoking. He passed away shortly after finishing his last book, *My America*, which I believe was his best ever. When I finished reading the book, which came out after his death, I felt sad and angry that, because of tobacco, we'd never read another book by this remarkable historian.

## Gambling

Some people gamble because they are looking for a shortcut to wealth. Usually it is a shortcut to financial ruin instead. Gambling can leave you broke, ruin your reputation, and if you get involved with the wrong people, it can take your life. When you gamble, the odds are stacked against you in every way possible. If you have any doubts about that, I suggest you take a drive down Las Vegas Boulevard and take a long, hard look at the billion-dollar hotels and casinos stretching for miles on both sides of "The Strip." Those luxurious hotels were built with the gambling losses of people like you and me.

## Pornography

I believe that a steady diet of sexually explicit material of any kind creates an addiction that is just as hard to escape as that caused by drugs or alcohol. People addicted to pornography find it difficult to have normal, healthy relationships with members of the opposite sex. They discover that impure thoughts lead to impure actions. And, they damage their relationship with God, who tells us to keep our thoughts pure. (See Philippians 4:8.)

## Illicit Sex

The world doesn't seem to see sexual purity as a virtue these days, but even though times may change, God's Word doesn't. He is the One who created sex, and the One who gave it to us as a special expression of love between one man and one woman who have committed themselves to each other for life in marriage. Any other use of sex is just plain wrong.

## Gluttony

Gluttony? Isn't that something out of the Middle Ages? Nobody talks about gluttony anymore. Maybe not, but more than half of all adult Americans are overweight, and it is a serious problem. Being overweight causes all kinds of health problems. Furthermore, even though gluttony may seem outdated, it is still a sin—especially in a world that produces more than enough food to feed all its inhabitants, but where children in Africa still starve to death every day. God expects us to take the best possible care of our bodies, and you can't do that by gobbling down tons of junk food.

## Money

I've already mentioned what the Bible says about the love of money, that it is "the root of all kinds of evil" (2 Timothy 6:10). There are many people who will do anything at all for money—lie, cheat, steal, and even kill. Our prisons are full of such men and women. There is nothing wrong with money in and of itself. Money is a means to an end. It provides us with a way to take care of the people we love. It gives us an opportunity to further God's kingdom. Money pays for shelter, food, medicine and other necessities. But if you lose sight of money's purpose and start loving it, you're headed for big trouble.

## Gentleness

*And the servant of the Lord must not strive;*
*but be gentle unto all men, apt to teach, patient.*
—2 Timothy 2:24 KJV

Is it really possible to be gentle and powerful at the same time? Absolutely! Some of the most powerful men and women I've ever known had a very gentle spirit. I think, for example, of former President Ronald Reagan. Former Canadian Prime Minister Brian Mulrooney said this about him: "Ronald Reagan always conducted himself with a great amount of courtesy. I never saw him be rude to anyone, though some were rude to him. I never saw him react in anger at a high-level meeting, nor did he throw his weight around. He always spoke softly. He knew how the American people wanted a president to act, and that is exactly what he did."

Another person who was extremely gentle yet powerful in a different way was a diminutive Roman Catholic nun by the name of Mother Teresa. She exuded gentleness. She rarely spoke above a whisper, and yet she was the instrument of God's grace and power to transform thousands of lives and open the world's eyes to the plight of those who live in desperate poverty.

Jesus said, "Blessed are the meek, for they will inherit the earth" (Matthew 5:5). The meek are those who understand that you don't have to be loud, angry, and demanding to make a difference in the world. They don't shy away from what needs to be done, but they do it with a gentleness and humility that draws others to them.

As I look around it's easy to see that we are not living in gentle times. Everything seems to be about toughness, power, and aggression. Many of the most popular movies are full of violence. It's the same with music. And, of course, movies and music are merely a reflection of what's going on out there in the real world.

Criminals seem to be increasingly violent. Hardly a day goes by that we don't hear about a terrorist attack somewhere in the world. Teenage gang members are killing each other with such frequency in some cities that police departments have set up special task forces to deal with the problem.

In the midst of this increasingly aggressive and violent world, God calls His people to be gentle. This is one important way we can be "salt and light" for America.

### Self-Control

*The worst ruler is the one who cannot rule himself.*
—Marcus Porcius Cato,
The Elder Roman Statesman

As football coach Lou Holtz said, "Self-discipline is an individual's greatest asset." Thomas O'Shaughnessy put it this way: "No man is free until he conquers himself." And Aristotle said, "The hardest victory is the victory over self."

The Book of Proverbs says, "Like a city whose walls are broken down is a man who lacks self-control" (Proverbs 25:28). That is so true! History is full of stories about people who ruined themselves because they never learned self-control. Mozart gave the world some wonderful music but died at a very young age because he did not take proper care of his body. The brilliant composer literally worked himself to death.

History also tells us about men and women who changed our world because they exercised discipline in every area of their lives. One of those who immediately comes to mind is inventor/statesman Benjamin Franklin. Franklin was constantly writing himself lists to keep himself headed in the right direction. One of those lists contained the following:

- Temperance—Eat not to dullness, drink not to elevation.

- Silence—Speak not but what may benefit others or yourself. Avoid trifling conversations.

- Order—Let all things have their place. Let each part of your business have its time.

- Resolution—Resolve to perform what you ought. Perform without fail what you resolve.

- Frugality—Make no expense, but do good to others or yourself. Waste nothing.

- Industry—Lose no time. Be always employed in something useful. Cut off all unnecessary action.

Another list well worth emulating is from preacher Jonathan Edwards:

- Resolved, to live with all my might while I do live.

- Resolved, never to lose one moment of time, to improve it in the most profitable way I can.

- Resolved, never to do anything which I should despise or think meanly in another.

- Resolved, never to do anything out of revenge.

- Resolved, never to do anything which I should be afraid to do if it were the last hour of my life.

Can you imagine what a wonderful world this would be if we all demonstrated a mature, self-controlled attitude in everything we do? That type of world has to start somewhere. It might as well begin with you and me!

# CHAPTER EIGHT

# TAKE RESPONSIBILITY

# FOR YOUR ACTIONS

*The buck stops here.*
—President Harry S. Truman

Sometimes it seems that we are living in a world full of victims. Everyone has a problem and somebody to blame for their problem. However, people of character understand that they alone are responsible for their actions.

Think about this for a moment. The first law of physics tells us that every action brings about an equal and opposite reaction. In other words, everything you do has consequences attached to it. This is not limited to the physical realm. It is also true in spiritual matters, for the Bible says, "A man reaps what he sows" (Galatians 6:7).

If you drink and become an alcoholic, you have no one to blame but yourself. If you smoke cigarettes and develop lung cancer, that is cause-and-effect in action. Nobody is responsible for what you do but you.

Admittedly there are many things we can't control. We can't control the weather. We can't control the family into which we are born. We can't control the passage of time. Sometimes we can't control much of anything except our attitude, but if we all took responsibility for the things we can control, our society would instantly change for the better.

In the Old Testament Book of Joshua, chapter 24, we find a great story about the importance of responsibility. After Joshua had succeeded Moses as leader of the Israelites, he led them to victory after victory over their enemies. In chapter 24, Joshua was old and knew he didn't have much longer to live. He also knew that the Israelite nation was at a crossroads. They would either move forward and become a great people, or they would be swallowed up by the surrounding cultures and gradually disappear. Based on past experience, he couldn't have been very optimistic.

The situation called for decisive action, and Joshua took it. He brought the leaders of the nation together and, in effect, drew a line in the sand. He said, "Choose for yourselves this day whom you will serve...But as for me and my household, we will serve the Lord" (Joshua 24:15).

The people responded passionately: "We too will serve the Lord, because He is our God" (Joshua 24:18). That was a pivotal moment in the history of the Jewish people.

We could sure use some Joshuas in this day and age! I believe that one of the reasons so many American companies get into trouble is because they have no Joshuas sitting on their boards of directors. No one issues a stirring call to responsible behavior. Nobody draws a line in the dirt and says, "We're going down the wrong road and we've got to get this thing turned around."

Why? Because it isn't always popular to do the responsible thing.

But it is always necessary.

Writing about Joshua's challenge to his countrymen, Pastor Bill Hybels says, "People have to make calculated decisions; they have to make tough, often costly choices, and leaders are often the catalysts for those heroic decisions." He added, "More and more, we leaders must take responsibility for leading people to decision points concerning important life issues."

America needs people who are willing to stand up and take responsibility for their actions. She also needs men and women who are willing to see that they are at least partly responsible for the actions of others. For example, if I know that a crime has been committed and I don't go to the proper authorities, I can be charged as an accessory to the act. I also believe that if I know someone who is engaged in improper behavior, it's my responsibility to do something about it. At the very least, I need to be willing to confront the guilty party.

I don't want to see America become a nation of snoops and snitches, but neither do I want us to become a nation of cowards. We must not be a people who are unwilling to get involved, who turn and look the other way when we see something wrong because we don't want to bother anyone. Here are some things we can all do to grow in responsible behavior:

- Quit playing the blame game.
- Take responsibility for our own actions.
- Learn to delegate responsibility to others.
- Seek accountability.
- Have clear objectives.

### Quit Playing the Blame Game

*Leadership consists of nothing but taking responsibility for everything that goes wrong and giving your subordinates credit for everything that goes right.*
—Dwight D. Eisenhower

In *The Devil's Dictionary*, Ambrose Bierce defines *responsibility* as "a detachable burden easily shifted to the shoulders of God, fate, fortune, luck, or one's neighbor. In the days of astrology it was customary to unload it upon a star."

It is always extremely difficult to accept the blame for something—especially when it is not entirely your fault. Nobody knows that better than the owner, general manager, or coach of a professional sports franchise. The general public doesn't understand that they are bound by budget restraints and a league salary cap. They won't cut you any slack if the guy you took first in the draft is injured in training camp and misses the entire year. They don't care if there are other factors that hinder a team's performance. They just want you to win—and now!

Do you know what? They have a right to expect that. After all, winning is what professional sports is all about. When we aren't winning, we have to take the heat—and the blame. Dick Vermeil, who coached the St. Louis Rams to their only Super Bowl victory and who now coaches the Kansas City Chiefs, has said that when his team doesn't play well, he is the one who takes the blame. He doesn't point fingers at his players, even when they make mistakes on the field. He believes that when a team—any kind of team—messes up, it's time for the leader "to stand up and say, 'Listen, I screwed up.' Never blame the players. You want them to assume the responsibility on their own. I know if a player walks up to me and says, 'Hey, Coach, I blew it,' he's going to get better."

That reminds me of Ralph Houk, a big, strong veteran of World War II who managed the New York Yankees to several championships in the 1960s. Houk was a tougher-than-nails, no-nonsense kind of guy. According to Jon Miller, who is now play-by-play announcer for Sunday Night Baseball on ESPN, "Ralph was the kind of guy who, when you looked at him, you had this uncontrollable urge to salute." Houk was tough on his players—in private. He worked them hard, but when something went wrong in a game, he was always there to take the blame.

Miller recalls in particular a game during the early 1980s when Houk was managing the Boston Red Sox. In a tie game with the bases loaded in the ninth inning, catcher Gary Allenson tried to pick a runner off first base. His wild throw went into right field, and the Red Sox lost the game as a result. According to Miller, when reporters gathered around Houk after the game to get his response, he said, "I don't know what I was doing out there. I ought to be fired for even thinking about that play. I owe my guy an apology. I'm the one who told him to do it, and it didn't work out."

The truth was that Allenson had called the play, but Houk was the leader, and he believed that he should bear responsibility. No wonder his teams won so many games, and no wonder his players loved him!

During World War II General Dwight David Eisenhower was responsible for planning the D-Day invasion of France that took place on June 6, 1944. Eisenhower knew that thousands of young soldiers would most likely be killed in the assault. He also knew that the invasion would be a pivotal point in the war against Nazi Germany. Success would be a tremendous boost to the Allied cause, but failure would be a crushing blow.

In the hours prior to the attack, as rain splattered on the windows outside, Eisenhower sat down at a small table and wrote out—by hand—a press release to be used if the attack should be repelled. He wrote:

> Our landings have failed...and I have withdrawn the troops. My decision to attack at this time and this place was based upon the best

information available. The troops, the air, and the Navy did all that bravery and devotion to duty could do. If any blame or fault attaches to the attempt, it is mine alone.

Eisenhower had made up his mind in advance that he was going to bear full responsibility for whatever happened. He wasn't going to put the blame on his advisors, bad weather, superior Nazi strength, or any other contributing factor. It was his responsibility and his alone.

I am reminded of another story about Ronald Reagan, this one concerning General Colin Powell. Powell tells of a cabinet meeting during Reagan's administration wherein a new policy was being discussed. Powell, along with several of Reagan's cabinet members, had written the new policy, and the president strongly disagreed with it. Even so, he respected the other men's points of view and was willing to yield to them in the matter. Thus, the policy was adopted.

Within a few weeks, the policy had proven to be a failure. A press conference was called to discuss the situation, and one reporter asked Reagan, "Was this policy formed by you, or was someone else responsible for creating this mess?"

Without skipping a beat Reagan responded, "Absolutely it was my idea. But I'll tell you something about this old dog. I might make a mistake one time, but I'll never make the same mistake twice."

Author Terry Felber says, "With that, he protected the reputations of his cabinet and General Powell." He adds, "General Powell remembers standing in the pressroom with tear-filled eyes, determined to serve President Reagan the rest of his life." It's been said that a good leader takes more than his share of the blame and a little less than his share of the credit. God, give us more leaders like that!

## Take Responsibility for Yourself

*You have brains in your head.*
*You have feet in your shoes.*
*You can steer yourself*
*Any direction you choose.*
—Dr. Seuss

Former New York Mayor Rudy Guliani has always kept a small sign on his desk. The sign bears two words: "I'm responsible." Says Guliani, "Throughout my career, I've maintained that accountability—the idea that the people who work for me are answerable to those we work for—is the cornerstone, and this starts with me." He goes on to say, "Nothing builds confidence in a leader more than the willingness to take responsibility for what happens during his watch. One might add that nothing builds a stronger case for holding employees to a high standard than a boss who holds himself to an even higher one. This is true in any organization, but it's particularly true in government."

As former British Prime Minister Margaret Thatcher once said, "We are all responsible for our own actions. We simply cannot delegate the exercise of mercy and generosity to others." Even though I agree with

Mrs. Thatcher, I also know that people have been making excuses for their behavior and refusing to accept responsibility for their actions since shortly after creation.

The first recorded excuse in history is found in the third chapter of Genesis. That's where Adam, after eating the forbidden fruit, points at Eve and says, "She made me do it" (Genesis 3:12 Pat Williams' Paraphrased Version)! Actually, Adam tried to pin the blame on God, reminding the Creator that Eve was "the woman you put here with me" (Genesis 3:12).

Humankind hasn't changed very much since that terrible day. Most of us are still looking for someone to blame for our problems. However, it wasn't a good idea thousands of years ago, and it's not a good idea today.

Some people complain that they would be doing better in life if only they hadn't been born...black...white...male...female...into a poor family...into a rich family...into a big family...into a small family...to parents who were too strict...to parents who were too lenient...to parents who were alcoholics...and on and on and on. We would all be much better off if we focused on what we can do because of what we *have*, instead of what we *can't* do because of what we *don't have*.

During the Civil War General Ulysses S. Grant was critized by other military leaders who found fault with his decisions and complained that he drank too much. On one occasion Lincoln responded to charges about Grant's drinking by saying, "Then find out *what* he's drinking so I can send my other generals a case."

On another occasion Lincoln said of Grant, "He doesn't ask me to do impossibilities for him, and he's the first general I've had that didn't." He went on to explain, "When any of the rest went out on a campaign, they'd look over matters and pick out some one thing that they were short of, and that they knew I couldn't hope to give them, and then tell me they couldn't win unless they had it."

Before setting out on his Virginia campaign in 1864, Grant wrote Lincoln, "Should my success be less than I desire and expect, the least I can say is the fault is not with you." Like Eisenhower after him, he knew that he alone was responsible for the success or failure of his troops.

Napoleon Bonaparte once responded scornfully to a question about the circumstances facing him. "Circumstances?" he snorted. "What are circumstances? I make circumstances." Arrogant? Perhaps. But there is truth in his words. I believe that we are all in God's hands, and that we are subject to His will. I also believe that God desires the best for His people. It is not God who holds us back. We hold ourselves back by refusing to take responsibility for our actions—and refusing to take action.

Is there something you've always dreamed of doing but never had the nerve to try? Today is the day to begin working toward the fulfillment of that dream! I urge you to take a few moments right now to think about where you want to go and what it's going to take to get there. (We'll talk about this when we get to the importance of setting goals.) Let yourself dream big! Get out a piece of paper and write it all down.

Tim Hansel writes in his book, *Life's Greatest Lessons*: "The good news is that the best season of your life can be ahead of you, no matter what your age or circumstances...if you choose to make it so...because 90 percent of your potential is not only untapped and unused but undiscovered. That's not just good news...it's incredible news!"

Here's something else to remember from playwright August Wilson: "You are responsible for the world you live in. It's not the government's responsibility. It is not your school's, your social club's, your fellow citizen's, your church's, or your neighbor's. It is yours...utterly and singularly yours."

I know I'm repeating myself here, but I feel I must say it again: Begin to pursue your dreams now! Don't be like the Anglican bishop, buried in London's Westminster Abbey, who has these words written on his tomb:

> When I was young and free, and my imagination had no limits, I dreamed of changing the world. As I grew older and wiser, I discovered the world would not change, so I shortened my sights somewhat and decided to change only my country. But it, too, seemed immovable. As I grew into my twilight years, in one last, desperate attempt, I settled for changing only my family...those closest to me, but, alas! they would have none of it. Now, as I lie on my deathbed I suddenly realize: If I had only

changed myself first, I would have changed my family by example. From their inspiration and encouragement I would have been able to better my country and the world.

The lesson is a simple one. If you really want to change the world, the best place to start is with yourself!

## Learn to Delegate Responsibility to Others

*Few things help an individual more*
*than to place responsibility on him,*
*and let him know that you trust him.*
—Booker T. Washington

You can't make it to the top in any profession unless someone gives you a chance. No one can move from one level to the next unless someone higher on the corporate ladder is willing to say, "Here. I think you can handle this. Why don't you take a shot at it?" That's the first reason why it is important to delegate responsibility and authority to others. It gives them a chance to grow.

Another reason why it's important to learn to delegate responsibility is this: If you try to do everything all by yourself, you'll eventually kill yourself! Just about everyone has the need to delegate some responsibility. For example, parents should delegate responsibilities to their children, and the responsibilities should get bigger as they grow older.

Small children may be given the responsibility of dressing themselves. When they are a bit older, they may be charged with the additional responsibilities of making their beds and keeping their rooms clean and tidy. If you are a parent, I know what you're thinking. As the father of nineteen children, I can tell you that you're right! Your children *will* let you down from time to time. But that's no reason to quit delegating and decide that the only way things are going to get done around your house is if you do them yourself. You've got to keep trying. It's important for you and your children. Dear Abby said, "If you want your children to keep their feet on the ground, put some responsibility on their shoulders."

A wife needs to delegate some of the responsibility of managing the household to her husband. A husband needs to delegate some of the responsibility to his wife. It was Abraham Lincoln who said, "The worst thing you can do for those you love is the things they could and should do for themselves."

In a business office or any occupation there is almost always someone to whom you can entrust some of what you are responsible for. If the person you have entrusted let's you down, then find someone else to do the job.

Jesus Christ is a wonderful example of the importance of delegating responsibility to others. He picked twelve rag-tag men who didn't seem to know where their lives were headed and turned them into dynamic leaders who helped to change the world in a few short years. Think about the men Jesus chose: a tax-collector, a radical who wanted to overthrow the Roman government,

181

some professional fishermen, and several other men who, as far as we know, had not distinguished themselves in any way. Yet Jesus saw potential in each one of them and gave them the responsibility to be leaders in the kingdom of God.

Did Jesus ever get discouraged and feel like these guys just weren't up to the task He was giving them? I'm sure He did. It took three years of intensive training for them to even begin to understand why Jesus had chosen them and what His ministry was all about.

Imagine how He must have felt when James and John came to Him and asked if they could be second in command when He took control of Israel. (See Mark 10:35-39.) After all He had taught them about the importance of servanthood and humility, they still argued about which one of them would be the greatest in His kingdom. (See Mark 9:33-37.) After all He had taught them about God's love and compassion, Peter wanted to call fire down from heaven to destroy some unbelievers. (See Luke 9:54.)

When Jesus asked them to pray with Him in the Garden of Gethsemane, they all went to sleep. (See Matthew 26:39-45.) When Jesus was arrested, they all scattered like so many scared sheep, even though they had just promised Him that they were ready to die with Him. (See Mark 14:50.) And during Christ's trial, Simon Peter denied three times that he knew Jesus, cursing and swearing to prove his point. (See Matthew 26:74.)

Through it all, Jesus never gave up on them. I like the way pastor Bill Hybels puts it: "He knew that, in the not-too-distant future, He would be handing over the leadership of the New Testament Church to them. He had to make sure that He chose people with the potential to assume that responsibility. After Jesus identified all twelve, He very quickly moved into an intense time of investing into their lives. He spent time with them. He taught them. He nurtured them. He confronted them. He motivated them. He rebuked them. He inspired them. Then, months later when He knew the time was right, He moved into the third phase of leadership development. He entrusted them with real ministry responsibility and coached them into effectiveness. His plan worked marvelously, and it's worth emulating."

I agree whole-heartedly with Ronald Reagan, who said, "When necessary, tasks must be delegated...without responsibility being abdicated." Certainly there are risks involved in delegating responsibility to others, but there are also tremendous gains to be made. For example, Jim Burke, CEO at Johnson & Johnson, encourages his people to be willing to take risks. He got that attitude from General Johnson, one of the founders of the company.

Burke remembers: "I developed a new product that failed badly. General Johnson called me in, and I was sure he was going to fire me. Johnson said to me: 'I understand you lost over a million dollars.' I can't remember the exact amount. It seemed like a lot then. I said, 'Yes, sir. That's correct.' So he stood up and held out his hand. He said, 'I just want to congratulate you. All business is making decisions, and if you don't make decisions, you won't have failures. The hardest job I have is getting people to make decisions. If you make that same decision again, I will fire you, but I hope you make lots of others, and that you understand there are always more failures than successes in any business.'"

Don't get discouraged if you fail at something or if someone to whom you delegate responsibility fails at something. Failure is often the stepping-stone to success, and it may take five or six failures before success is finally achieved.

Thomas Edison was the driving force behind dozens of amazing inventions, but he is best remembered for one in particular, the electric light bulb. Before he finally got it right Edison failed one thousand times in his attempt to create the light bulb! Again, success often springs from failure.

### Seek Accountability

*Every choice you make is a building block of your life.*
*Every act, every word, every decision becomes a part*
*of you. The way you see and respond to the world*
*you live in is the result of the choices you have made.*
*So, in a sense, not only do your choices make you*
*who you are, but they, in effect, make your world,*
*because the world that you see is the world you live in.*
—John Marks Templeton

Of course he's right, but how can we be sure that we are making the correct decisions to shape ourselves and our world in the best possible way?

*Part of having a strong sense of self is to be accountable*
*for one's actions. No matter how much we explore*
*motives or lack of motives, we are what we do.*
    —Janet Geringer Woititz, Writer

One of the most important answers to this question is that we all need someone to hold us accountable—someone who is honest, wise, and mature. To whom should you be accountable? Someone you trust with your deepest thoughts and secrets. Someone who isn't afraid to speak up, forcefully, when they see you on the verge of making a wrong decision or heading off in the wrong direction. Someone who understands your weaknesses and can empathize with you when you are facing temptation.

Some people have put together accountability groups to meet with them once every week or so, and I think this is a great idea. The "accountability factor" is one reason why groups like Weight Watchers work so well. And, of course, it is one of the dynamics in twelve-step programs such as Alcoholics Anonymous. Having other people around you to hold you accountable for your actions can help you become the best person you can possibly be. As director Rob Reiner says, "Everybody talks about wanting to change things and help and fix, but all you can do, ultimately, is to fix yourself, and that's a lot. If you can fix yourself, it has a ripple effect."

If you have a person or a group to hold you accountable for your actions, you are much more likely to act in good, responsible ways. C. S. Lewis said, "Every time you make a choice, you are turning the central part of you—the part that chooses—into something a little different than what it was before. Taking your life as a whole, with all your innumerable choices, you are slowly turning this central thing either into a heavenly creature or into a hellish creature."

Where do you find the people you can report to? Just about anywhere. But I would look especially for men and women whom you know have a high degree of spiritual maturity. In his book, *It's About Time*, Ken Smith, president of Christian Stewardship Ministries, gives three excellent suggestions for developing a system of accountability.

The first is to form a relationship with one other person and submit your decision-making process to them. Smith does give a word of caution. "This approach requires a very high degree of commitment for you and the other person. It is also subject to the greatest danger. You run the risk of letting the relationship disintegrate into a controlling process...But if the relationship retains a Christ-centered balance, it is probably most likely to produce real Christlike change in your life."

The second approach to accountability is through membership in a group in which the various members hold each other responsible. Smith says that in such a group, "There needs to be a willingness to assume responsibility for each other and to take the initiative in discovering each other's shortcomings."

The final way to establish a system of accountability is to have a one-on-one relationship with several different people—sort of a system of checks and balances. Author Smith says, "The greatest liability of this approach is that it requires a great deal of your time."

## Have Clear Objectives

*The number one reason why people
do not set goals is that they have not yet
accepted personal responsibility for their lives.*

—Tommy Newberry

Another important way we can grow in responsibility is to figure out where we want to go in life and then set goals to get there. How important are goals? The story is told about an art professor who died and met Saint Peter at the pearly gates of heaven. "Saint Peter," he asked, "there's something I've always wanted to know, and I was wondering if you could give me the answer."

"Certainly," the apostle smiled.

"Who was the greatest artist of all time? Michelangelo, DaVinci, Monet, or perhaps Van Gogh?"

Peter shook his head. "None of them," he said. "The greatest artist of all time was Henry Jones."

"Henry Jones!" exclaimed the art professor. "But I knew Henry Jones. He was a janitor at the university where I taught."

Peter sighed and said, "Yes, that's true. God gave him more talent than any of the others you mentioned, but he never picked up a paintbrush. He had so much innate ability, but he never learned to use it."

As this story suggests, some people sit and dream about what they want to be in life, but they never take the first step to get there. As writer Neil Eskelin says, "You were created with natural abilities and an internal compass that guides you toward a particular focus for your life. That's only the starting point. The next step is yours. You have an obligation to expand that potential to its ultimate destiny."

Here are a few important things to know about goals:

- Goals should be in writing. Putting them down on paper makes them real, and makes it more likely that they will be truly pursued.

- Each goal should be concise. Preferably, no more than one sentence. Being concise forces us to think about what the goal really is—and to make it more direct and to the point. A goal that rambles all over the place is really no goal at all.

- Larger goals must be broken down into smaller goals. For example, if your ultimate objective is to write an Academy-Award winning screenplay, your first goal might be to take a class in screenwriting. Or, if you've already done that, it might be to sit down tonight and write the first three pages of your script.

- Goals must be reasonable. It would be ridiculous for someone who is tone deaf to set a goal of singing in the Metropolitan

TAKE RESPONSIBILITY FOR YOUR ACTIONS

Opera. Your goals must be consistent with your desires and abilities.

• Goals should have a deadline attached. This is important because a deadline keeps you moving forward. A friend of mine told me that he used to set goals all the time but rarely took any action toward accomplishing them. It was only when he attached a deadline to his goals—a deadline he took seriously—that he really began to move toward his lifelong dreams.

Listen to what Pastor/Author Chuck Swindoll says about the importance of having objectives for your life. "A piano sits in a room gathering dust. It is full of the music of the masters, but in order for such strains to flow from it, fingers must strike the keys...trained fingers, representing endless hours of disciplined dedication. You do not have to practice. The piano neither requires nor demands it; however, if you want to draw music from the piano, that discipline is required. You do not have to pay the price to grow and expand intellectually. The mind neither requires nor demands it; however, if you want to experience the joy of discovery and the pleasure of plowing new and fertile soil, effort is required. Light won't automatically shine upon you, nor will truth silently seep into your head by means of rocking-chair osmosis. It's up to you. It's your move."

God has put it into you to do great things, but it remains up to you to do them!

Why should you set goals for yourself? As psychologist Abraham Maslow says, "If you plan on being anything less than you are capable of being, you will probably be unhappy all the days of your life."

When you have clear-cut goals for yourself and live each day in accordance with those goals, you will find what author Stephen Covey writes, "How different our lives are when we truly know what is deeply important to us, and keeping that picture in mind, we manage ourselves each day to be and to do what really matters most."

Next, we're going to talk about the importance of starting...persevering...and finishing. But first, I want to leave you with a poem written by Dan Baker.

You can love me
    but only I can make me happy.
You can teach me
    but only I can do the learning.
You can lead me
    but only I can walk the path.
You can promote me
    but I have to succeed.
You can coach me
    but I have to win the game.
You can even pity me
    but I have to bear the sorrow.
For the gift of Love
    is not a food that feeds me.
It is the sunshine that nourishes
    that which I must finally harvest for myself.

So if you love me
    don't just sing me your song.
Teach me to sing,
    for when I am alone
I will need the melody.

# CHAPTER NINE

# NEVER GIVE UP

*Just don't give up trying to do what you really
want to do. Where there is love, inspiration,
and hard work, I don't think you can go wrong.*
—Ella Fitzgerald, Singer

As far back as he could remember, the young man
had always wanted to be a writer. He spent almost every
moment of his leisure time working on his craft, and
the more he wrote, the more his passion for writing
grew. Now, in his twenties, it was becoming apparent
that he had chosen the wrong profession. He had received more than 120 rejections from various publishers. Their form letters said, "Thanks, but no thanks,"
and decorated the walls of his apartment. Not one of
his short stories or novels had been accepted, but the
young man continued to write and look for new publishers who might be interested.

On the 123rd try, someone finally said yes. A publisher was willing to take a chance on *This Side of Paradise.* That's when the writing career of F. Scott
Fitzgerald finally got going. Fitzgerald is now universally

regarded as one of the best American writers of the twentieth century. During the height of his popularity he talked about how he felt in the early days, when he was getting one rejection after another. "I didn't get discouraged," he said. "I got angry. The rejection motivated me to keep going."

If we both had the time and the pages to spare, I could tell you hundreds of stories about people like Fitzgerald, who persevered in the face of adversity and kept right on going until they finally finished—and won—the race. They demonstrated a spirit that could not be stopped or defeated, and they made the world a better place through their contributions.

Here's another reason why American society has been rocked by scandal: *Too many people have forgotten that persistence pays off.* They don't want to do what it takes to change the world. They'd rather go around an obstacle than through it. Instead of fighting their way up the white-water rapids, they want to float down the lazy river in an inner tube and still achieve success. In Moses' day they would have been among those who didn't want to go on to the Promised Land, but who desired instead to go back to Egypt because life was so much easier there!

## Keep on Keeping On

I know of two instances where discouraged writers threw manuscripts in the trash. In both cases the authors' wives retrieved the literary works and urged their husbands to keep going. The first manuscript was *The*

*Power of Positive Thinking,* by Dr. Norman Vincent Peale. Just think how many lives that book has changed for the better! It never would have happened if Mrs. Peale had thought, "Well, maybe he'll get that crazy book-writing idea out of his head now." Thankfully she didn't.

The second book that nearly died before it was born was *Carrie,* which became a runaway bestseller for Stephen King. King has gone on to have an amazing career—he's certainly given me my share of goose bumps and chills—but it almost didn't happen.

One more story. When the great composer, Sergei Rachmaninoff, fled Russia during the revolution of 1917, he left his entire lifetime of work behind, along with all of his other possessions. He wound up in Sweden, unknown and penniless. Instead of brooding about the misfortunes that had befallen him, he rebuilt his fortune by returning to the concert stage.

Before he felt that he was ready to perform publicly, he practiced for several weeks—spending more than sixty hours per week at the piano. Over the next twenty-five years, Rachmaninoff gave hundreds of concerts in Europe and the United States and kept on composing. By the time of his death he had firmly established his reputation as one of the great pianists and composers of the twentieth century.

The lesson to be learned from all this is that it is so important not to give up. But in order to follow my advice, you have to be doing something in the first place! That's why, in the rest of this chapter, I want to discuss the importance of getting started, persevering, and finishing what you started.

## Get Started

*The most difficult thing is the decision to act;*
*the rest is merely tenacity.*

—Amelia Earhardt

If there is something you want to do, but you're afraid to get started, take a lesson from the bamboo tree. Do you know how much the bamboo tree grows during the first year after it is planted? Zero. How about the second year? Zilch. For four years there is no visible evidence that anything has been planted. Anybody who didn't know better would say, "You wasted your time when you planted that thing. It's dead."

In reality, the bamboo plant is just getting ready for an incredible growth spurt in year five. How incredible? Ninety feet in thirty days. No, that's not a misprint. The plant grows three feet a day for an entire month. At the end of that time, it reaches as high as a nine-story building.

It's really true that great things can and often do come from the smallest beginnings. As the old Chinese proverb says, "A journey of one thousand miles begins with a single step." But it's up to you and me to take that step. We have to start somewhere. And we have to start, period.

Singer Joan Baez said, "Action is the antidote to despair." In other words, it's counter-productive to sit around worrying about the condition of your life, your marriage, or the world today. Concern is only worthwhile if it motivates you to do something about the situation.

Off the top of my head, I can't tell you how many books I've written. In every instance, however, the hardest thing has always been getting started. You have no idea how long I can sit and stare at a blank monitor screen or a blank legal pad. I know perfectly well what I want to say. Sometimes I feel so passionate about my subject that I have a burning sensation in my chest, and yet it is the hardest thing in the world to put those first few words on paper.

Once I get started, the words, sentences, paragraphs, and pages usually come pouring out of me. In fact, before a manuscript is finished, I usually have to go back through and find places to cut because I've written too much! I'm telling you this because I want you to know that if you are afraid to take that first step, you're not alone. You have plenty of company. Starting out on any endeavor can be extremely difficult.

The Bible has quite a bit to say about getting a fresh start in life. For example, it tells us that, "We were therefore buried with him [Christ] through baptism into death in order that, just as Christ was raised from the dead through the glory of the Father, we too may live a new life" (Romans 6:4). In 2 Corinthians 5:17, Paul writes, "Therefore, if anyone is in Christ, he is a new creation; the old has gone, the new has come!"

In 1914, when Thomas Edison was sixty-seven years old, his laboratory and factory burned to the ground. Much of his life's work was destroyed in the fire, and Edison also lost a tremendous amount of money. The damage was estimated at $2 million, but only $238,000 was recoverable through insurance. (And $2 million in 1914 would be worth somewhere around $100 million today.)

Edison's son, Charles, who was then twenty-four years old, wrote of finding his father standing in the chilly air of the winter night, watching the fire, seemingly exhilarated by the spectacle. Charles wrote: "My heart ached for him. He was sixty-seven years...no longer a young man...and everything was going up in flames. When he saw me, he shouted, 'Charles, where's your mother?' When I told him I didn't know, he said, 'Find her. Bring her here. She will never see anything like this as long as she lives.'"

The next morning, as Edison walked through the rubble and debris left by the fire, he said, "There is great value in disaster. All our mistakes are burnt up. Thank God we can start anew." Three weeks later he unveiled the first phonograph.

Edison was right. There *can be* great value in a disaster if we allow it to spur us to bigger and better things. If we learn from it, the scandal that has rocked the American economy over the past couple of years could be a very good thing. It gives us the chance to start over, on both a corporate and personal level. Now is the time for all of us to start:

- Being completely honest in everything we do.

- Striving for integrity in all things.

- Demonstrating an "old-fashioned" work ethic.

- Developing a mature attitude.

- Learning what it means to be responsible.

It's also time to take the first step toward the life that we've always wanted to have, a life in which we use our God-given potential to the fullest, a life that pleases us because we know it is pleasing to God.

Perhaps you remember the old cliché from the 1960s: "Today is the first day of the rest of your life." Kind of corny, huh? But also very true. Whatever you want to do, start it today and not tomorrow! As the Bible says in 2 Corinthians 6:2, "Now is the time of God's favor, now is the day of salvation." There is only one time to start anything, and that time is now!

### Don't Quit

*Most of the important things in the world have been accomplished by people who kept on trying when there seemed to be no hope at all.*

—Dale Carnegie

I love stories about people who made it to the top in their professions despite being told by others that they just didn't have what it takes. Over the years I've collected dozens of these stories, which show the importance of dogged persistence and perseverance. Take a moment to see if you can match the quotes that some so-called experts had to say about these future celebrities: Diana Ross, Cher, Jack LaLane, Sally Jesse Raphael, Ray Charles, and Arsenio Hall:

**A** "You should get a job as a secretary. We're not using women."

**B** "Working out with weights causes athletes to lose their speed and agility. Bodybuilding causes hemorrhoids and hernias."

**C** "You can't play the piano, and God knows you can't sing. You'd better learn how to weave chairs so you can support yourself."

**D** "Television isn't ready for a black talk-show host. You can forget it."

**E** "You have a nice voice, but it's nothing special."

**F** "You will never make the cover of Vogue because you do not have blonde hair or blue eyes."

If you matched Quote A with Sally Jesse Raphael, you're correct. That's what she heard when she sought a job in broadcasting after her graduation from Columbia University.

Quote B was aimed at Jack LaLane, when the fitness guru burst upon the scene in the 1950s. Today every major league sports franchise has a weight room, and the last I heard of LaLane, he was in his eighties and still performing amazing feats of strength.

The victim of Quote C was Ray Charles. His teachers obviously didn't know that Charles would go on to sell millions of records and become one of America's all-time favorite singers.

I'm sure you knew right away that Quote D was directed at Arsenio Hall before he went on to host a successful late-night talk show for Paramount.

Quote E was uttered by a teacher as she rejected Diana Ross for a singing role in a high-school production. Little did she know she was passing up the future leader of The Supremes, the Motown trio which had more than twenty-five top-forty hits, including twelve that made it all the way to number one.

That leaves one celebrity and one quote. Quote F is attributed to photographer Richard Avedon, who was speaking to Cher. Like the others quoted above, he was wrong. Not only did Cher appear on the cover of Vogue, but when she did the magazine sold more copies than ever before.

If people are picking on you and telling you that you don't have what it takes, you're in very, very good company!

In the mid-1980s, when I joined the effort to bring NBA basketball to Orlando, there were plenty of people who said we didn't have a chance. Some people still thought of Orlando as a small town, overshadowed by other Florida cities such as Miami, Tampa, and Jacksonville. Orlando did not have a single major-league franchise, so it was not a proven sports area.

It is not my nature to get down. You can ask my administrative assistant, Melinda Ethington, about that. She sees me everyday when I'm not out on the road with the Magic or on a speaking tour, and she'll tell you that I can outrun the Energizer Bunny nine days out of ten. But there were times during Orlando's fight for a franchise when I felt as if all hope was gone. I tried not to show it, but negativity hung in the air so thick that I could actually feel it weighing me down. Every time we cleared what we thought would be the final hurdle, someone threw another roadblock in our way.

I can't begin to count the times we were pumped full of excitement and then quickly deflated in a single afternoon. Nevertheless—along with just about every-one else connected with the effort to bring profession-al basketball to Orlando—I kept on keeping on. And I will never forget the day when the big phone call came from NBA Commissioner David Stern. Even then, the struggle wasn't over.

The league wanted us to sell ten thousand season tickets before the start of our first season, which was one year away. Most of the teams in the league had nowhere near that number of season ticket holders, but it was a NBA mandate, and we had to do it. That meant I had no time to relax. I had to get back out on the lecture-circuit and start selling tickets.

There were times during that next year when I thought we were never going to make it. We finally reached our goal just a few minutes prior to our dead-line, when a gentleman came in and bought the last four tickets! As we found out in Orlando, it is truly amazing what you can accomplish if you don't give up.

Remember, if you are in a correct relationship with God, He is on your side. As the Bible puts it, "If God is for us, who can be against us?" (Romans 8:31). You're always on the winning team if you're aligned with God. It doesn't matter if Saddam Hussein, Osama

Bin Laden, and satan himself are coming against you, accompanied by every terrorist in the world and every demon from the depths of hell. If God is on your side, the bad guys don't stand a chance.

I think of a story from the Old Testament, when the king of Aram sent troops to arrest the prophet Elisha. The king was angry because he was fighting a war with Israel, and Elisha the prophet always knew exactly what the enemy was up to. (Israel didn't need spies.) The Bible says that when Elisha's servant went out in the morning, he saw that an army of horses and chariots had surrounded the city. Frightened, he ran back to Elisha's house, crying

> *"Oh, my Lord, what shall we do?" the servant asked.*
>
> *"Don't be afraid," the prophet answered. "Those who are with us are more than are with them."*
>
> *And Elisha prayed, "O Lord, open his eyes so he may see." Then the Lord opened the servant's eyes, and he looked and saw the hills full of horses and chariots of fire all around Elisha.*
>
> 2 Kings 6:15-17

I sometimes pray that the Lord will open my eyes so I can see all the ways He's helping me, even when it feels like things are stacked high against me. I pray that He will enable me to stay strong, positive, and focused on the task at hand, even when I'm surrounded by people who don't believe in me.

I know of two pretty good actors who were fired on the same day by Universal Studios because they couldn't act. Studio bosses told one of the young men that he was too ugly to be a movie star. Oh, he might get some roles as a criminal-type—a rapist or a mugger perhaps—but he would never be a leading man. The other fellow was given the news that nobody could get their eyes past his large Adam's apple long enough to notice whether he could act.

The final insult came when the two men left the studio parking lot for the last time. The names on their parking spaces had already been painted over!

Do you have any idea who these guys were?

The ugly guy was a fellow by the name of Burt Reynolds.

The guy with the huge Adam's apple was Clint Eastwood.

When Wilma Rudolph fell ill with polio at the age of four, doctors told her parents she would be paralyzed for life. When she was twenty, she won three gold medals at the 1960 Olympics. Now a member of the Olympics Hall of Fame, Rudolph says her remarkable recovery came about primarily because of her mother, who massaged her legs and "encouraged me to gain movement in any way I could."

For months nothing happened. Then one day Wilma managed to wiggle her toes. It took years before she was walking with the aid of braces, but by the time she was twenty she was the fastest female runner in the world.

My friend Peter Lowe, who holds annual SUC-CESS conferences in Orlando, told me how he went about getting President Reagan to speak at one of those conferences in the late 1980s. He said, "I wrote a letter to President Reagan. He didn't write back to me. I wrote him another letter. He ignored me. I wrote him another letter. His secretary wrote back saying President Reagan regretfully declined my offer to speak at one of our seminars. I ignored the secretary. I wrote another letter. And another. And another.

"I called the president's office every week. I'd call and say, 'Hi, this is Peter Lowe. Has President Reagan decided to speak for me yet?' The secretary would say, 'Hi, Peter. The answer is the same as last week. The president is not going to speak for you.' I'd call the next week, 'Hi, this is Peter Lowe.' She'd say, 'Hi, Peter. The president is not going to speak for you.' It finally came down to a weekly two-word dialogue. I'd say 'Hi.' She'd say 'No.' We'd both laugh and I'd call back the next week. This went on for four years...until President Reagan finally decided to speak for me."

Persistence pays off!

When Frank Deford, one of my favorite sports writers, was a guest on my radio show, we got to talking about the qualities that set champions apart from (also-rans). He said, "Here's what I noticed about champions. It doesn't come easy to them, but they hang in there and don't give up."

I was recently talking to a young man named Mike Zanca, who is an intern with the Orlando Magic. After his sophomore year at UCLA, Mike decided he wanted to go into the sports business and began looking for a job as an intern. Over the next few months he received eight hundred rejection letters. That's not a typo. Eight hundred! He saved all of them and has them stored in two big plastic notebooks.

Finally, last fall Mike got a call from our marketing department, saying that an intern position had opened up—if he was willing to pay for his own move from California to Florida. Mike accepted our offer, and I predict that this young man is going to go far. Talk about persistence!

In Matthew 7:7, Jesus says, "Ask and it will be given to you; seek and you will find; knock and the door will be opened to you." Bible scholars have told me that this passage would be more faithful to the original language if it read, "Keep on asking...keep on seeking...keep on knocking."

This is consistent with Jesus' parable of the unjust judge, as recorded in chapter 18 of Luke.

> *"In a certain town there was a judge who neither feared God nor cared about men. And there was a widow in that town who kept coming to him with the plea, 'Grant me justice against my adversary.'*
>
> *"For some time he refused. But finally he said to himself, 'Even though I don't fear God or care about men, yet because this widow keeps bothering me, I will see that she gets justice, so that she won't eventually wear me out with her coming!'"*

Luke 18:2-5

Jesus expects His followers to have a "never-say-die" attitude. Here are a few ways you can develop such an attitude, even when the odds seem to be stacked against you:

## Use Positive Self-Talk

Do you remember the story of *The Little Engine That Could?* He kept repeating to himself, "I think I can! I think I can!" He kept repeating those words as he pulled a heavy load to the top of a steep hill. Finally he got to the point where he was saying, "I know I can! I know I can!" I know it's a children's story, but many of the stories we learned when we were kids are full of great truths based on universal experience. It's too bad that when people grow up, they forget so many of the truths they learned when they were children.

Some people are harder on themselves than any one else would be, like Groucho Marx, who said he wouldn't belong to any organization that was crummy enough to ask him to be a member. Or they feel like Woody Allen, who said, "My one regret in life is that I am not somebody else." I asked one guy why he kept putting himself down and he said, "I beat myself up so nobody else will."

That reminds me of the joke about the guy who asked his friend, "Why is it that everybody takes an instant dislike to me?"

"Because it saves time," his friend replied.

Or perhaps you've heard the one about the woman who whined, "The whole world is against me!"

"The whole world isn't against you," her friend comforted her. "Some people don't even know you yet."

The unfortunate thing is that if you go around beating yourself up, other people are going to start believing what you say about yourself—and they'll start beating you up too.

Please be nice to yourself! Say good things to yourself about who you are, and remind yourself that you have strengths and abilities nobody else has. Tell yourself over and over again that God loves you. If negative, self-deprecating thoughts begin to play in your brain, change the channel. Positive self-talk will make you feel good about yourself, and I believe it will also increase your energy level and strength—and thus help you achieve your goals.

## Don't Worry About Being a Plodder

I've had people tell me that they feel like giving up because they're just not as sharp or quick as others. But you know what? I'd be willing to bet that most of those other people are faking it! Once again, we've forgotten what we learned in childhood, namely that slow and steady wins the race. Remember the tortoise and the hare? I've heard that story about a million times, and the tortoise always wins!

As I mentioned before, my main talents are perseverance and hard work. I find that when you work harder and longer, you're going to get where you want to be. Television personality Sally Jesse Raphael was pretty close to the mark when she said, "The only talent is perseverance."

Calvin Coolidge said: "Press on! Nothing in the world can take the place of persistence and determination. Talent will not; nothing is more common than unsuccessful people with talent. Genius will not; unrewarded genius is almost a proverb. Education will not; the world is full of educated derelicts. Persistence and determination alone are important."

One of the reasons so many people lose their shirts in the stock market is that they are out to make a fortune overnight. They think they can figure out exactly when to buy and when to sell. Some do make a fortune that way, but my personal opinion is that this is due more to luck than anything else. By far, the majority of people who do well in the market are those who make investments in stable companies and then leave them alone over a substantial period of time. They may be seen as plodders, but over thirty years or so persistent plodding can bring amazing results.

### Don't Let Failure Deter You

Remember the story of the *Three Little Pigs*?

The first pig built a house of straw, but The Big Bad Wolf huffed and puffed and blew it all down.

"He ran for shelter to his brother's house of sticks, but some huffing and puffing on the part of old Big Bad brought this house tumbling down, too."

This time, the two homeless pigs ran to safety in a third brother's house, made out of bricks. And this time, the house proved to be wolf-impervious. All of his huffing and puffing was to no avail and presumably, the three brothers lived happily ever after. Along the way, they taught us a few things about learning from our failures and mistakes. If you build a house of straw, and that doesn't work, build one out of sticks. And if that doesn't work, try bricks. Every failure provides a chance to learn and improve, until you get things right!

Jean Driscoll has won the Wheelchair Division of the Boston Marathon six times. I've run in twenty-seven marathons, and I can tell you that it's not easy to run non-stop for twenty-six-plus miles. I can't even begin to imagine pushing myself in a wheelchair for that distance. By the time you reached the finish line, your arms would be so sore and tired, they'd probably feel like they were going to fall off!

Yet Jean Driscoll has done it again and again and turned in some incredible times along the way. How did she do it? She says, "Some people think that successful persons are born that way. I'm here to tell you that a champion is someone who has fallen off the horse a dozen times and gotten back on the horse a dozen times. Successful people never give up."

**Albert Einstein** could not speak until he was four years old.

**Ludwig van Beethoven's** music teachers called him hopeless.

When **F. W. Woolworth** was twenty-one, he got a job in a store but was not allowed to wait on customers because he "didn't have enough sense."

**Walt Disney** was fired by a newspaper editor because he didn't have any good ideas.

Failing at something does not mean your idea wasn't a good one, or that you did something wrong. Everyone alive has failed at one time or another. As Jean Driscoll said, successful people keep getting back on the horse that bucked them off.

Michael Blake, who wrote one of my favorite movies, *Dances with Wolves*, wants you to know, "Your dreams can come true. I'm living proof of it. I left home at seventeen and had nothing but rejections for twenty-five years. I wrote more than twenty screenplays, but I never gave up."

### Don't Listen to What Others Say

I'm sure you've heard the old fable about the father and son who were going on a long-journey with a donkey. At first the son rode the donkey while the father walked. When they heard people say, "Look at that lazy boy, taking it easy while his father walks," they changed positions. Then people said it wasn't right for the father to be riding while his son walked along in the hot sun. So...they decided that they would both ride. That only caused people to complain that the two men were mistreating the poor donkey. At that point, they got off and began carrying the donkey.

The story goes on for a while, but the point of it is that if you let other people's comments and attitudes dictate what you're going to do, you're not going to be able to do very much of anything. Some people will complain about everything and anything. Their favorite line is: "It can't be done." And their next-favorite line is, "We've never done it this way before." (Which means, of course, that the *old* way of doing things was the *only right* way of doing things.) That's why I love this poem, quoted by former Secretary of Education William Bennett in his *Book of Virtues*:

> The man who misses all the fun
> Is he who says "It can't be done."
> In solemn pride he stands aloof
> And greets each venture with reproof.
> Had he the power he'd efface
> The history of the human race.
> We'd have no radio or motor cars,
> No street lit by electric stars;
> No telegraph or telephone,
> We'd linger in the age of stone.
> The world would sleep if things were run
> By men who say, "It can't be done."

## Draw Strength From God's Word

Tremendous strength can be gained from time spent meditating on and soaking in God's Word. There are so many promises of God's help and blessings upon His people. One of my personal favorites is found in Isaiah 40:30-31: "Even youths grow tired and weary, and young men stumble and fall; but those who hope in the Lord will renew their strength. They will soar on wings like eagles; they will run and not grow weary, they will walk and not be faint."

Another wonderful promise is found just three chapters later.

*"Fear not for I have redeemed you; I have summoned you by name; you are mine.*

*When you pass through the waters, I will be with you; and when you pass through the rivers, they will not sweep over you. When you walk through the fire, you will not be burned; the flames will not set you ablaze.*

*For I am the Lord, your God, the Holy One of Israel, your Savior."*

Isaiah 43:1-3

The Bible is full of similar encouragement for God's people. How could anyone feel like giving up when they have that kind of power in their soul? PRAY! PRAY! PRAY!

Dwight L. Moody was the Billy Graham of his day. During the latter years of the nineteenth century, he was arguably America's best-known preacher, preaching before thousands of people every Sunday. Mr. Moody made it a practice of praying for an hour every morning— except when he had an especially busy day. Then he prayed for two hours. You say, "That doesn't make sense." It does in God's economy.

### Finish What You Start

*It is easy to start on a task, but God needs people*
*who can last on the job when the going gets difficult,*
*and who can finish what they set out to do.*
—Halford E. Luccock

When Henry Ford was still at the helm of the company that bears his name, an ambitious young employee sought him out and asked, "How can I make my life a success?"

Ford didn't even have to think about it. He quickly answered, "When you start something, finish it."

Imagine you are working in a pit crew at the Indy 500, and your driver is in the lead for the first 499.5 miles. There you are, surrounded by a cheering throng of nearly two hundred thousand people, about to see your guy cross the finish line first and zoom right on into racing history. Instead, he suddenly pulls off the track into the infield, climbs out of his car, stretches nonchalantly, and says, "That's enough."

"What do you mean, that's enough!" you shout. "Are you crazy?"

"Crazy?" he echoes. "That's no way to talk to me after the way I drove today. I was in the lead most of the way."

You'd think the guy had blown every one of his gaskets—and you'd be right. Because he didn't finish the race, all his good driving won't mean a thing. As racer Rick Mears said, "To finish first, you must first finish."

You have to keep going until you cross the finish line! You need to be able to say, along with the apostle Paul, "I have fought the good fight, I have finished the race" (2 Timothy 4:7). In order to get to the point where you can say this, you need to live as he did, "Forgetting what is behind and straining toward what is ahead, I press on toward the goal to win the prize" (Philippians 3:13-14).

I have an acquaintance who never finishes anything she starts. When I first met her, she was studying to get her license to sell real estate. She lost interest and decided to sell insurance instead. That was boring, so she decided to look into a franchising opportunity. Of course, that never got more than an inch or two off the ground. Those are just three of the ten or more goals she's had in the time I've known her. Just think of all the time she's wasted spinning in circles!

Composer John Williams, who has written the music for scores of movies, including the *Star Wars* series, once explained his success by saying, "Tenacity will get those of us who are not geniuses but mere mortals, over the finish line." And basketball Hall of Famer Oscar Robertson said, "The moment you admit to yourself that you're beaten, you're beaten. It's that simple."

If you're having a tough time right now, that probably means you're doing something right. You're not going to face that much adversity if you just drift along with the current, going wherever life takes you. It's only when you're battling your way to higher ground that life becomes difficult. It's only when you speak up for what's right and speak out against what's wrong that you're going to have opposition.

I'm sure you've heard it said that the darkest hour is just before the dawn. I also believe that the road is roughest just before the finish line. That's why I love the sign I once saw in the office of former college basketball coach Lefty Dreisell: "If the going's getting easier, you ain't climbing."

Earlier in this chapter I asked you to match some negative comments with the people they were aimed at. Here are a few more cutting remarks directed at people who wouldn't quit until they had crossed the finish line of success:

A New York publisher to James Michener: "You're a good editor with a promising future in the business. Why would you throw it all away to try to be a writer. I read your book. Frankly, it's not that good." The publisher was referring to *Tales of the South Pacific*, which earned Michener a Pulitzer Prize.

Advice given by several consulting firms to Gustave Leven regarding his plans to market Perrier water in the United States: "You're foolish to try to sell sparkling water in the land of Coca-Cola drinkers."

Attorneys for Mary Kay Ash, just before she began marketing the cosmetics line that made her a billionaire: "Liquidate the business right now and recoup whatever cash you can. If you don't, you'll wind up penniless."

Her accountant to Estee Lauder: "It's a cut-throat business and you've got no chance of success."

His parents to Arnold Schwarzenegger: "How long will you go on training in a gym all day and living in a dream world?"

Finally, in 1946 a young singer by the name of Ray Charles got a chance to audition for bandleader Lucky Millinder in Orlando. Charles put everything he had into his performance. After the last notes faded, they sat in silence for a moment. Then Millinder said simply, "Ain't good enough, kid." Charles cried for days after that. But then it occurred to him that it didn't matter what anyone else said or thought as long as he believed in himself and kept on trying. Today Ray Charles is one of the most recognized singers in the world—and has been for more than forty years.

But I wonder: Whatever happened to Lucky Millinder?

CHAPTER TEN

# SEEK HUMILITY

*Humility is the essence of life.*
—Frank Wells

I love this definition of humility from Andrew Murray: "Humility is perfect quietness of heart. It is to expect nothing, to wonder at nothing that is done to me, to feel nothing done against me. It is to be at rest when nobody praises me, and when I am blamed or despised. It is to have a blessed home in the Lord, where I can go in and shut the door, and kneel to my Father in secret, and am at peace as in a deep sea of calmness, when all around and above is trouble."

Rich DeVos is one of the richest men in America. Yet I've noticed that whenever he meets someone for the first time, he always says, "Tell me about you." He doesn't want to talk about himself. That's a humble spirit. Humility is not an absence of strength or self-confidence. Being humble is not the same as being wimpy.

**David Robinson** of the San Antonio Spurs has been one of the best players in the National Basketball

Association for many years. He is also a humble, unassuming man who gives God the glory for His success. The same can be said of St. Louis Rams' quarterback **Kurt Warner**, Kansas City Royals' powerful young first baseman **Mike Sweeney**, and softball hero **Dot Richardson**. The lives of these four athletes show that humility and strength go together very well.

When I'm traveling—which is often—I usually ask the driver who picks me up at the airport if he's had many celebrities in his car. If so, I ask him which ones he remembered the most. In December in Dallas, Buddy told me that he'd driven at least fifteen hundred celebrities over the years. When I asked about his favorites, he thought for a moment and then began rattling off their names, "**Jimmy Stewart, Kirk Douglas, David Halberstam, Suzanne Somers, and Mickey Mantle**."

"What made those five special?" I asked.

"They were all just regular people," he said. "No big-time stuff with them. They were down-to-earth and easy to be with." Wow! Wouldn't that be a great epitaph: "He was down to earth and easy to be with." That's so much better than, "He was a self-important jerk!"

Another driver, Robert, told me that his favorite passenger was actor **Tom Hanks**. He described Hanks as "a very regular guy. No plastic. In fact, he wouldn't get in the stretch limo because it was too showy. He made us get a regular sedan."

A flight attendant told me that her most memorable passenger was **Debbi Fields** of Mrs. Field's Cookies.

"She is sweet and humble," she told me. "She was very friendly to everyone. She is just a regular person, and her five daughters were just the same."

Here are some of the other stories I've heard over the years.

Jerry, in San Diego, told me his favorite passengers were **Dustin Hoffman** and **Joan Rivers**, "because they were so down-to-earth, understanding, and pleasant to be around."

In Orlando Gabriella's favorite had been **Jacquelyn Kennedy Onasis**. Why? "Because she was so nice to me. A very sweet lady."

Gordon in San Francisco told me it was easy to pick his favorite. "**The Smothers Brothers**. Having them in the limo was like a live TV show. They were just regular, fun guys."

Bud in Charlotte singled out **Arnold Palmer** and **Graham Nash**, of the rock group Crosby, Stills and Nash. "Both of them," he said, "made you feel comfortable and had no lofty view of themselves."

In Los Angeles John said singer **Patti LaBelle** was his favorite: "She was great. Lots of fun...She and her friends wanted to get pizza. The crowd recognized her and insisted that she sing to them. With the jukebox as background, she belted out a song, right in the restaurant."

One driver told of running into **Oprah Winfrey** in downtown Chicago a few days after he had given her a ride in his limo. Even though he was out of uniform and didn't have his nametag on, she came over to say hello and called him by name.

Jim told me that he had been a driver for **Geraldo Rivera** on two occasions, about three years apart. He told me, "On the second time, he greeted me by name, and I wasn't wearing a nametag." He also told me that actress **Ann Jillian** had dinner sent out to him from an expensive restaurant in Chicago, after he turned down her invitation to dine with her and her family.

And here's one of the most amazing stories of all. Jim picked up **Ray Charles** and took him to the airport in Chicago, where the singer was catching a plane to Pittsburgh. On the way to the airport, Jim mentioned that he had a brother in Pittsburgh who was blind. Charles responded by asking for the brother's address and phone number. That night, Jim's brother called, and said, "You'll never guess who I had lunch with today." The answer, of course, was Ray Charles!

I have dozens of similar stories, but I just wanted you to know that it is possible to be famous, powerful, and still humble. Somehow we've picked up the idea that only bad people make it to the top. It just isn't true. You don't have to step on other people, knife them in the back, or throw your weight around to be a success in business or any other area of life. Leo Durocher said, "Nice guys finish last," but he didn't know what he was talking about. Nice, humble guys (and girls) can finish first as well—they *can* make it into positions of power.

Ralph Waldo Emerson said, "A great man is always willing to be little."

I talked to a man the other day, who told me about an experience he had with the great Christian leader Torry Johnson. Johnson, as you may know, is the founder of Bible Town in Boca Raton, Florida. The man I spoke to told me that he and Johnson were walking across the grounds there, and Johnson kept stopping to pick up scraps of paper and other pieces of litter.

"Why are you doing that?" my friend asked. "You have people here who are hired to do that job."

Johnson bent down and picked up another piece of trash. As he straightened up he said, "If you're too big to do the little things, you're too little to do the big things." What a great way to think about it!

Now, being humble does not mean that you lie about yourself. You're not demonstrating humility if you say, "I can't sing," when you're the first tenor in the Metropolitan Opera. You're not showing humility if you describe yourself as a "plain Jane," when you've just won the Miss America pageant. It's not being humble to describe yourself as an average golfer if you're Tiger Woods.

Humble people appreciate their own positive attributes, but they realize that those attributes are, for the most part, gifts. As someone has said, "Humility is not denying the power you have but admitting that the power comes through you and not from you."

A humble attitude can be developed through practice. You can practice humility when you're at work, when you're at home with your family, or just about any other place you can think of. Here are five important ways practicing humility can change your life. People who practice humility.

- Are admired by other people.
- Are exalted by God.
- Bend, but rarely break.
- Don't care who gets the credit.
- Learn to live in the present moment.

### Humble People Are Admired by Others

*People with humility don't think less*
*of themselves—they just think about themselves less.*
—Norman Vincent Peale

Humble people are admired because they really listen to other people. They consider others' points of view. They are encouragers. They enter every situation with a desire to build up and not to tear down. They are not loud, demanding, and full of themselves. They may be confident, but they are never stuck-up or snobby.

I would modify Dr. Peale's quote above to say that humble people don't think less of themselves—they just think more of others. As the apostle Paul wrote to the church at Philippi: "Do nothing out of selfish ambition or vain conceit, but in humility consider others better than yourselves. Each of you should look not only to your own interests, but also to the interests of others" (Philippians 2:3-4).

Brooks Robinson was an outstanding third baseman for the Baltimore Orioles during the 1960s and 1970s. So good, in fact, that he was recently named one of the greatest third basemen of the twentieth century. I can still remember watching Brooks' outstanding play in the 1971 World Series, where he dominated the entire series with one outstanding play after the other. He looked like a human vacuum cleaner out there. Nothing got past him!

Since then I've had the privilege of playing with Robinson in some old-timer benefit games, and his humility impresses me just as much as his talent. He not only gives autographs freely but engages his fans in friendly conversation. He asks where they're from. He asks if they're Orioles' fans, and if so, how they became Orioles' fans. He asks where they went to school, what they do. He almost makes people feel as if he's their fan instead of the other way around.

Typically when I asked him how he felt about being named one of the greatest third basemen of the century, he said that it was a great honor, but that he felt embarrassed, "because there were so many great players at that position." When you are genuinely humble, people just naturally like you and feel comfortable with you.

Elizabeth Dole says that during the Reagan Administration, most of the people she escorted into the Oval Office to meet with the president seemed to be extremely nervous and self-conscious. But after a few minutes of conversation with Mr. Reagan, they were relaxed and totally at ease. Humble people, whatever their station in life, are easy to be around.

I remember talking with actress Linda Evans, when we were both appearing on the same radio program in Birmingham, Alabama. She seemed genuinely interested in what I had to say. She made eye contact, smiled, and asked questions. I was completely impressed by her humble, down-to-earth manner, and I've told just about everyone I know about my meeting with her. This is an excellent example of what I mean when I say that humble people are admired by others.

Ester de Waal wrote, "Humility...comes from humus, earth, and simply means that I allow myself to be earthed in the truth that lets God be God and myself His creature. If I hold on to this, it helps prevent me from putting myself at the center; instead, it allows me to put God and other people at the center."

It is true that fame has a way of stealing humility from people. Former television evangelist Jim Bakker wrote about the way he was changed by being on TV: "It is so easy to get swept away by popularity. Everybody loves you, cars are waiting for you, and you go to the head of the line. That is the devastation of the camera. It has made us less than what God has wanted us to become."

Do I have some stories about famous people who were arrogant, demanding, and rude? Of course, but I won't share them, because it's not my intention to criticize anyone. Besides, everyone has a bad, angry day once in awhile. I'll even admit that there've been a few times when I haven't demonstrated a humble attitude. As I get older, I'm striving to make sure those self-centered moments happen less and less.

As a boy I went to school in Wilmington, Delaware, with Ruly Carpenter, whose father, Bob, owned the Philadelphia Phillies. Ruly and I were good friends, and his dad was like a second father to me. After I graduated from college, Mr. Carpenter signed me to a professional contract, and I spent a couple of years as a catcher in the Phillies' farm system.

When I was twenty-four, he sent me to Spartanburg, South Carolina, as general manager of the Phillies Class A franchise there. My second year in Spartanburg, we won our league championship, at one point capturing an amazing twenty-five games in a row. We also set a franchise attendance record, drawing 173,000 paying customers in a city of fewer than 50,000 people. I was twenty-six years old, and just about as full of myself as I could possibly be, having not yet surrendered my life to Christ.

At the end of that great season, I was summoned to Philadelphia and interviewed about the possibility of becoming general manager of the Phillies' AA franchise in Reading, Pennsylvania. I remember that I interviewed with the biggest names in the Phillies' organization. Bob Carpenter was there, of course, as was General Manager John Quinn and Farm Director Paul Owens.

The move to Reading would have been a step up in my career, but it wasn't enough of a step to suit me. I turned the job down, and I did it in an arrogant way, bringing the interview process to an abrupt stop.

Today, nearly forty years later, I'm ashamed and embarrassed when I recall the way I acted on that occasion. Truthfully, it wasn't even until I got back to Spartanburg that I realized what I had done. Four months later, when I was home for Christmas, I went to see Bob Carpenter and tried to tell him how sorry I was for the way I acted. He finally accepted my apology, but that was the end of my upward mobility in the Phillies' organization. Although things have worked out great for me in the NBA, I still wish I had handled that interview differently.

You may or may not be famous, but you can still treat people in such a way that they will have fond and lasting memories of you. That's what it means to be humble. As someone has said, there are two kinds of people in the world. The first kind walks into a room and says, "Here I am!" The second kind walks into a room and says, "Ah! There you are.

### God Exalts Those Who Humble
### Themselves Before Him

*Humble yourselves before God*
*and He will lift you up.*

—James 4:10

When God chose Moses to lead the children of Israel out of Egypt, Moses protested that he wasn't a

good public speaker and urged the Lord to find someone else. (See Exodus 4:10-12.)

When the angel of the Lord told Gideon that he
had been chosen to liberate the nation of Israel from
the Midianites, Gideon protested that he was the least
important member of the weakest family in Israel. (See
Judges 6:15.)

When Saul was chosen to be the first king of Israel,
he was so embarrassed that he tried to hide. (See
1 Samuel 10:20-22.)

David was a young shepherd boy when the prophet
Samuel anointed him as the next king of Israel. (See
1 Samuel 16:1-13.)

Mary was a simple, teenage peasant girl when she
was chosen to give birth to the Messiah. (See Luke
1:46-48.)

Are you beginning to see a pattern here? God lifts
up and exalts those who are humble in heart. Jesus told
his disciples that whenever they were invited to a marriage feast, they should not take the seats of honor.
After all, He said, "a person more distinguished than
you may have been invited. If so, the host who invited
both of you will come and say to you, 'Give this man
your seat.' Then, humiliated, you will have to take the
least important place" (Luke 14:8-9).

Jesus continued, "But when you are invited, take
the lowest place, so that when your host comes, he will
say to you, 'Friend, move up to a better place.' Then
you will be honored in the presence of all your fellow

guests. For everyone who exalts himself will be hum-
bled, and he who humbles himself will be exalted"
(Luke 14:10-11).

During His earthly ministry Jesus demonstrated
amazing humility. He was the Son of God, and yet He
was born in a barn. When he rode into Jerusalem on
Palm Sunday, he was riding a lowly donkey instead of a
proud, white stallion. You can't get much more humble
than that!

There is a passage in the Talmud in which the
prophet Elijah is asked, "How will we recognize the
Messiah when He comes?"

Elijah answers, "He will be sitting among the lepers, bandaging their wounds."

There's a reason why so many of Jesus' contem-
poraries did not recognize Him as the Messiah. They
expected the Messiah to enjoy the company of princes
and kings. Instead, He spent his time healing lepers
and telling the poor about God's love. They expected
Him to come with a flourish of trumpets and a blaze of
glory, but He came riding on a long-eared, braying
donkey.

Jesus was humble, but He wasn't a wimp. He knew
who He was and was sure of His authority. He drove
moneylenders out of the temple. He got right in the
Pharisees' faces when it was necessary. He was a powerful person, but He was humble.

Jesus epitomizes what Alan Ross calls, "the humble
leader." Ross says, "Humility means knowing and using

your strength for the benefit of others, on behalf of a higher purpose. The humble leader is not weak, but strong...is not pre-occupied with self, but with how best to use his or her strengths for the good of others. A humble leader does not think less of himself, but chooses to consider the needs of others in fulfilling a worthy cause. I love to be in the presence of a humble leader because they bring out the very best in me. Their focus is on my purpose, my contribution, and my ability to accomplish all I set out to accomplish."

Jesus told us that the man or woman who wants to be the leader of all must strive to be the servant of all, and He wasn't being ironic. He was telling it the way it is. Humility—real humility—is not weakness. Being humble does not mean you are a wimp. It simply means that you have a proper view of yourself. Humility starts with an understanding that all of your abilities, strengths, and positive attributes are a gift from God.

On the other hand, Proverbs 16:18 tells us that "pride goes before destruction," and it's true. I love what author Rick Warren says about humility: "Self-importance, smugness, and stubborn pride destroy fellowship faster than anything else. Pride builds walls between people; humility builds bridges. Humility is the oil that soothes and smoothes relationships. That's why the Bible says, 'Clothe yourselves with humility toward one another" (1 Peter 5:5). The proper dress for fellowship is a humble attitude. The rest of that verse says, 'because "God opposes the proud but gives grace to the humble."' This is the other reason we need to be humble:

Pride blocks God's grace in our lives, which we must have in order to grow, change, heal, and help others."

Warren goes on to give four very practical ways we can develop humility.

- Admitting our weaknesses.

- Being patient with others' weaknesses.

- Being open to correction.

- Pointing the spotlight at others.

### Humble People Bend But Don't Break

*Don't take yourself too seriously. Don't think
that you should somehow be protected
from the misfortunes that befall other people.*
—Robert Louis Stevenson

Another way of stating this is that humble people are able to laugh at themselves. They don't take themselves too seriously. They understand that, no matter how important you may think you are, sooner or later you'll get the props knocked out from under you.

In 1972 Don Shula coached the Miami Dolphins to a perfect record, including a lopsided victory over the Washington Redskins in the Super Bowl. No other team in NFL history has ever won all of its games in a year.

Shortly after that incredible season ended, Shula and his wife Dorothy took a vacation to a small town in Maine. One night they entered a theater to see a movie, and the few people in the audience gave them a loud ovation. Shula held up his hands in a quiet gesture and assured the people in the theater that he was really just a normal guy, that he didn't expect special treatment, and so on.

He was quickly brought back down to earth when one of the patrons said, "We don't know who you are, pal. They just told us they wouldn't start the movie until they had at least twelve people in here, and you two put us over the top."

On his Inauguration Day in 1976, Jimmy Carter had a similar experience. Carter admits that he was swelling with pride as he heard the cheers of the crowds lining Pennsylvania Avenue in Washington, D.C. He says that his press secretary, Jody Powell, had advised the president and his family to try to avoid reporters on that hectic day because the situation seemed tailor-made for embarrassing goofs.

Carter's mother, Miz Lillian, wasn't having any of it, and angrily told Powell that she would talk to whomever she pleased. Sure enough, before the family got back to the White House, they were confronted by a television news team. The reporter thrust his microphone in Miz Lillian's face and asked, "Aren't you proud of your son?"

Carter remembers, "I moved very close to hear my mama's complimentary response, and Mama said, 'Which one?'" The former president laughs at the memory and says, "It kind of brought me down to earth, before I even got to the White House."

Comedian Mike Downey, who was Frank Sinatra's opening act for many years, tells of the time he and

Sinatra were together in a small café in Palm Springs, California. A woman came in because she wanted to hear a song on the jukebox, but the jukebox was broken.

"I'll sing for you," Sinatra offered.

"No thanks," she said, as she turned and walked out of the restaurant.

"She didn't recognize you," Downey said, trying to spare Sinatra's feelings.

The famous singer just laughed and said, "Maybe she did."

Sam Donaldson tells of the time that he and fellow television journalist David Brinkley were approached by a fan as they stood in line at an airport. The man didn't recognize Donaldson, but was very excited to see Brinkley. "I watch you all the time," he said. "I think you're absolutely great."

"Thank you very much," Brinkley responded, a bit embarrassed by the fellow's adulation.

"Tell me," the man went on, "How's Chet?"

He was referring, of course, to Chet Huntley. Huntley, who had been Brinkley's broadcast partner, had died in 1974. Without missing a beat, Brinkley replied, "Well, about the same as usual."

Maybe the man wasn't such a big fan after all. Otherwise, he would have known that Huntley-Brinkley hadn't been a team for years. As author Paul Powell wrote, "Blessed is he who has learned to laugh at himself, for he shall never cease to be entertained."

David Brinkley tells of other occasions when he was given the opportunity to be entertained. For example, there was the time—when Chet Huntley was still alive—that Brinkley encountered a sweet, gray-haired woman who asked, "Aren't you Chet Huntley?"

Brinkley remembers, "I said yes because it really didn't matter anyway. We were like twins almost. She said, 'You are very good, but I cannot stand that idiot Brinkley.'"

Yes, well...

David Brinkley is in pretty good company. Following the Civil War, General Ulysses S. Grant was on his way to a reception in his honor when rain suddenly began to pour down. Grant politely offered a stranger a dry spot under his umbrella. Because Grant was not in uniform the stranger didn't recognize him. He told the general that he too was on his way to the reception, even though he thought Grant was vastly over-rated.

General Grant nodded in agreement. "I feel exactly the same way," he said.

That's humility!

Here's another one, and then we'll move on. Tonight Show host Jay Leno, one of the nicest people in television, tries to answer as many letters as possible, and sometimes calls people who have written him. On one such occasion, when he asked for Susan, the voice on the other end said she wasn't home and asked "Who's this?"

"This is Jay Leno."

"Well, this is her mother, what do you want?"

"She wrote me a letter," Leno replied.

There was a deep sigh on the other end of the line. "Yeah, well, she writes to every crackpot on TV."

As John Marks Templeton put it, "A humble attitude is a flexible one. Just as the tree and the building must sway with the wind, our agility in dealing with whatever life throws our way will be our strength." He goes on to say, "Humility is a strength that serves us well; it leaves us open to learn from others and to refuse to see issues and people only in blacks and whites."

### Humble People Don't Care Who Get the Credit

*Great people have little use for fame or notoriety.*
*They are consumed with productivity; not image.*
*They do not feel the need to project their self-worth*
*to anyone. They are content when the moment*
*calls for them to be little, ordinary, or*
*common...as long as the goal is achieved.*

—John Maxwell

I saw in the paper the other day that Yoko Ono is mad at Paul McCartney. Why? Because McCartney has rearranged the credits on some of the songs he wrote with John Lennon when the two were with The Beatles. According to Ono, Paul and John had an agreement that all of their songs would be credited to Lennon-McCartney, even the ones they actually wrote as individuals, such as *Yesterday*. But on a CD McCartney released after his 2002 tour of the United States, the songs are attributed to McCartney-Lennon.

If you're thinking, *Big deal*, so am I. Why does it matter to anybody whether it's Lennon-McCartney or McCartney-Lennon? Unfortunately, we live in a world where things like that do matter. Leonard Bernstein, the famous composer and conductor, was once asked to name the most difficult instrument to play in an orchestra. He answered quickly, "Second fiddle." How very true! (Incidentally, when Bernstein was a boy, his father hated the fact that he was interested in music and pressured him to give it up to go into the family business. Years later, when Bernstein senior was asked about this, he responded, "How was I to know that he was *Leonard Bernstein*?")

When Harry Truman was president, his secretary of state, George Marshall, came up with a $17 billion plan to rebuild Europe in the aftermath of World War II. Truman's advisors wanted him to call it, "The Truman Plan," but he wouldn't hear of it. He waved off the suggestion by saying, "It's amazing what you can accomplish when you don't care who gets the credit." It was "The Marshall Plan" which helped to repair the damage of war and thrust the United States into the role of a super power.

Don Fisher, CEO of the Gap says, "People's egos are a big problem in running a business. I haven't let my ego get in the way of anybody. I'd just as soon have other people get credit for stuff rather than me. If I were to take credit for all of it, it would be very discouraging to the guy who really did the work."

Multi-millionaire industrialist Andrew Carnegie said, "No man will make a great leader who wants to do it all himself or get all the credit for doing it." He also said, "I owe whatever success I have achieved, by and large, to my ability to surround myself with people who are smarter than I am."

### Humble People Live in the Present Moment

*Now listen, you who say, "Today or tomorrow we*
*will go to this or that city, spend a year there,*
*carry on business and make money." Why, you*
*do not even know what will happen tomorrow.*
*What is your life? You are a mist that appears*
*for a little while and then vanishes.*

—James 4:13-14

In his song, "Desolation Row," Bob Dylan mentions a character who dresses "with thirty pounds of headlines stapled to his chest." Do you know anybody like that? Somebody who believes their own press releases—aren't they annoying? Penn State football coach Joe Paterno said, "Publicity is like poison. It won't hurt you unless you swallow it."

Fame does things to people. So does power. And most of what it does is not good. It causes people to believe the flattering things others say about them and to think they deserve to be treated like gods and goddesses instead of ordinary human beings—which is what we all are.

I think it's fine to be proud of the things you've accomplished. But it's not fine to go around with your nose in the air, thinking you're better than everyone else because of something you did yesterday. A person who is truly humble knows that what's really important is how they are acting now, at this very moment.

Because the humble person lives realistically in the present moment, they will not waste someone else's time. They will do their best to be on time for appointments. They won't show up late for meetings. They understand that, because life is measured out in seconds and minutes, everyone's time is of equal importance.

George W. Bush's staffers remember how agitated their boss became when he was going to be late for an appearance during the 2000 presidential election. "Late is rude," he said. "Just rude! People are doing me a favor by coming out." That is a perfect demonstration of a humble attitude.

Another reason why humble people live in the present moment is that they understand that life is fleeting. The only time to do what must be done is now. This present moment is the only guarantee any of us has.

Author Mark Atteberry says it well: "It doesn't matter how many records you have set or awards you have won. It doesn't matter how vast your worldly kingdom is or how high you've managed to climb on the ladder of success. There's no getting around the fact that you are made of dust; not steel, and someday, if the Lord tarries in His return, you are going to die."

I realize that death is not a pleasant thing to contemplate, even for the Christian. However, remembering that our flesh is mortal should serve to keep us humble and focused on things that are really important in life.

There is a story about the late Dr. Albert Schweitzer that illustrates the importance of living in the present moment. Many years ago dozens of dignitaries and members of the media had gathered at a train station in Chicago to await Dr. Schweitzer's arrival. Schweitzer, who had dedicated his life to bringing life-saving medical help to the poorest of the poor in Africa, had just won the Nobel Prize. Excitement was in the air as the train squealed slowly to a stop, the doors opened, and the good doctor stepped out onto the platform.

He was instantly recognizable—tall (six-foot, four inches), with bushy hair and a large mustache. Dozens of flashbulbs exploded as government officials pressed forward to shake his hand and to tell him how happy they were to have him in their city. Schweitzer started to respond, but then his attention was captured by something going on behind them.

"Will you excuse me for just a moment?" he asked—and then strode right on through the assembled crowd. As everyone followed along behind him, Schweitzer hurried to the side of a frail elderly woman who was struggling with two suitcases that were much too heavy for her. Sweeping the suitcases up in his large hands, he escorted the lady on to her train. After politely wishing her a safe journey, he returned to the platform and apologized for keeping everyone waiting. Newspapers later quoted one of the government officials as saying, "That's the first time I've ever seen a sermon walking."

You know, I'd rather see a sermon than hear one any day. And I'd much rather be a sermon than preach one. How about you?

# CHAPTER ELEVEN

# SOMEONE IS WATCHING YOU!

*People do what people see. They forget*
*my sermons, but follow my footsteps.*
—John Maxwell

On their days off, some men head to the golf course. Others to the lake to do some fishing. Me? You'll almost always find me with my face in a book or magazine. I love to read. Recently, in *American Heritage* magazine, I came across a wonderful letter from a man named Rob Slocum.

Slocum remembers that way back in 1956, when he was six years old, he went to a baseball game at Ebbetts Field in Brooklyn. Rob was just getting over mononucleosis, and his father took him to the game as a special treat. What Rob didn't know was that his mother had written a letter to Rob's hero, Jackie Robinson, who played for the Brooklyn Dodgers. Mrs. Slocum had told Robinson that her son would be in the right-field stands, and it would be a tremendous thrill for him if the famous player would stop by and say hello.

Rob's father laughed when his wife told him about her letter. He said that celebrities like Jackie Robinson probably got dozens of requests like that every day. There was just no way they could respond to all of them. Nevertheless, he took his camera to the game that afternoon—just in case.

About fifteen minutes before the game started, Robinson came walking out of the Dodgers dugout toward the right-field stands. He stopped when he reached the warning track and called out, "Is there a boy named Rob Slocum up there?"

"That's me!" Rob shouted.

He jumped out of his seat and raced to the railing to shake his hero's hand, and Robinson handed him a ball that he and several of his teammates had autographed. As Rob's father snapped pictures with his little Brownie camera, Robinson explained that he had forgotten to bring the letter with him to the stadium that afternoon. He had to call his wife to get the boy's name and find out where he was sitting.

Today, nearly fifty years later, Attorney Rob Slocum still has the baseball Jackie Robinson gave him on that long-ago afternoon. He has never forgotten Jackie Robinson's act of kindness, which has been a tremendous influence throughout his life. He also has a letter Robinson wrote in response to his mother's thank-you note. It reads, in part,

> I guess if we, as ballplayers, realized the reaction the average fan gets out of meeting a ballplayer, we would react differently. I am

sure that most feel as I do, that we are only ballplayers, and don't quite understand what it may mean to young boys, and some adults as well. Your letter gave me a big kick...to know your reaction. Actually, it is such a little thing to do, and to get such a nice letter makes me aware of how much more it should be done. Thanks for making me realize this.

I always shake my head in disbelief when I hear a sports star defend his character flaws by saying, "I'm not a role model. I'm an athlete." I want to say, "Of course you're a role model! We're *all* role models!" That's especially true of anyone who is in the public eye—an athlete, an actor, a politician, or a celebrity of any sort.

Celebrity or not, everyone has a sphere of influence. Maybe you don't affect as many people as professional athletes and other celebrities do, but you might be surprised if you knew how many people are watching you and even copying your behavior. Your sphere of influence may include your children, your spouse, your brothers and sisters, your co-workers, your neighbors, your classmates, your teammates, your friends... the list could go on and on. What you do really matters for all of these people.

When he was a young man, Sidney Poitier had an experience that was quite different from what happened to Rob Slocum. Poitier remembers that he walked into a hotel lobby and saw a famous entertainer talking to some friends. Poitier stood quietly off to one side until there was a lull in the conversation. Then, at what he thought was an appropriate moment, he approached the star and asked for an autograph.

Poitier remembers: "He didn't say anything. He just looked at me with an annoyed look, like I was wasting his time. I was frozen. Finally, he reached out in a disparaging way and took my paper and pen, scribbled something and passed it back to me. I felt awful, awful awful." Poitier carried the sting of that rejection with him for a long time, and he vowed that he would never treat anyone that way. No wonder he has always been so approachable. "I am never too rushed to give someone an autograph—even if I'm hurrying to catch a plane," he says.

Sidney Poitier understands that even the little things he does may have a profound affect on someone else's life—for good or bad. He has chosen to make a conscientious effort to ensure that his influence is for good.

How about you? Have you made up your mind that you will strive to be a positive influence in every situation?

When Muhammad Ali was in his prime, he loved to run his mouth. He went on and on about how pretty he was, and how he was the best fighter who'd ever lived (which he very well may have been). But underneath all of that, he was and is one of the most accommodating people in the world of sports, as I know from personal experience.

A few years ago Ali was honored at a special event on the Disney property in Orlando. I had the good fortune to be sitting at a table not far from him and had two old photographs of me with the champ that I wanted to get autographed. I felt that would be asking a lot, though, because Ali suffers from Parkinson's disease, which has made it hard for him to write. When the opportunity presented itself, I slipped over, showed the photos to Ali's wife, Lonnie, and said, "I don't want to stir things up, but I'd love it if Muhammad could sign my pictures."

She looked at me as if I were nuts and said, "Go ask him." Ali was more than happy to sign my photos, although it must have taken him nearly five minutes to do so. By the time he was finished, others had seen what he was doing, and that opened the floodgates. Everyone wanted an autograph—and Ali signed until everyone was happy.

Why is Muhammad Ali so accommodating? Because when he was a young fighter, still known as Cassius Clay, he had a disappointing encounter with his hero, Sugar Ray Robinson, who acted bored and disinterested. Years later, Ali said, "I was so hurt. If Sugar Ray only knew how much I loved him and how long I'd been following him, maybe he wouldn't have done that." He went on, "I said to myself, right then, 'If I ever get great and famous and people want my autograph enough to wait all day to see me, I'm sure going to treat them different.'"

One of the best ways I know to change the world is simply to be a good influence. Here are five important things to remember:

- Someone is always watching.
- Be careful who you follow.
- Every action carries a message.
- Do your best all the time.
- Pay the price. It's well worth it.

### Someone Is Always Watching

*I believe that virtually every person is the most important leader to one other person in the world.*
—U. S. Attorney General John Ashcroft

Have you ever stopped to think about the people who are watching your actions as you go through an ordinary day? I'm not talking about the IRS, the CIA, or spies from some foreign country. I'm referring to:

Your children, if you have any.

Your spouse, if you're married.

Your brothers and sisters, and other relatives—perhaps even your parents.

Your neighbors.

Your co-workers or classmates.

The clerk at the dry-cleaning shop.

The waitress at the coffee shop where you have your lunch.

The other drivers on the road during the morning rush hour.

The other people in your carpool.

The cashier and bag boy at the grocery store.

Depending upon your personal situation, you may subtract some of these people from your list and add others. Nevertheless, my point remains the same. If you really stop and think about it, we all have contact with many people on an almost daily basis.

Every once in a while when I'm on the road, someone will come up to me and say something like, "There's something different about you. What is it?" When I answer that I'm a Christian, the response I usually get is something like, "Oh, that explains it!" Then they tell me that I just seem so happy...or nice...or that I've behaved in some other way that captured their attention.

I haven't said anything special. I certainly haven't tried to preach to anybody or handed out copies of "The Four Spiritual Laws." There was just something in my behavior that drew attention. I'm often left thinking, *I didn't even know that person was paying attention. I'm glad I wasn't acting like a jerk.*

My point in telling you this is not to brag about myself. I am certain that there have been times when I've drawn attention by acting rudely or indifferent. Like everyone else, I have my bad days. But I have become aware that people are watching all the time, even when I'm not aware of it.

Colin Powell tells his subordinates, "Always do your best because someone is watching." In other words, if you want to advance in your career, don't just put in your best effort when you know the bosses are watching. Put in your best effort all the time, because the bosses are *always* watching, whether you realize it or not.

Who's watching you? It may be your children or your neighbor's children. Whoever it may be, the little things you do can make a difference in that one life, and thus in the world at large.

I agree with columnist Ellen Goodman, who wrote, "I have never been especially impressed by the heroics of people convinced that they are about to change the world. I am more awed by the heroism of those who are willing to struggle to make one small difference after another."

A woman I know named Kathy recently received a letter from Jennifer, a little girl who used to live next door to her. Actually, Jennifer isn't a little girl anymore. She's a married woman with a little girl of her own—a baby just two months old.

For ten years while she was growing up, Jennifer lived next door to Kathy and became best friends with her daughter, Amy, who is just about Jennifer's age. Kathy admits she used to get exasperated because nearly every evening at dinnertime, her daughter would come and say, "Mom, can Jennifer eat with us tonight?"

Kathy didn't always have enough food for an extra guest, and some nights she was exhausted by the time she got home from work. But she almost always said okay anyway. Jennifer spent the night a lot too. Kathy even devoted one night a week to a club for the girls, which she called "Friends Forever." Together they sponsored a child through World Vision, and Kathy did her best to instill Christian values in them.

She was often discouraged because it didn't seem to be working very well—especially during those troubling, early teenage years. Eventually, the girls went their separate ways. Jennifer got married. Amy went off to college. And then the letter came out of the blue.

Dear Kathy,

I'm writing this letter to let you know that you have always been my hero. Thank you for everything you have done for me over the years. As I've watched you with Amy, I've always felt that she was lucky to have a mom like you, and I know that I am lucky to have you for a second mom. I have learned so much from you about being a mother and a friend. I just hope that as my little girl grows up, I can be the mother you have always been.

I love you,
Jennifer

You never know what influence you might be having on other people. Even if you feel discouraged or feel that you're making no impact at all, know that you are planting the seeds. You can trust God to cause them to bloom at the appropriate time.

One of my prize possessions is a letter my daughter Karyn wrote to me when she was a freshman at Indiana University.

> I couldn't have asked for a better dad to escort me through childhood. As I see the way some of my friends are treated by their fathers, I am even more grateful for your never-ending encouragement and motivation. I have notes that you've sent me hanging up in my room, and I don't think you know how much they mean to me...You have been the greatest father a girl could ask for!

It's not easy to share something like this letter because it's so personal. But it presents a great example of the way our actions can affect others, whether or not we realize it. If Karyn hadn't written that letter, I never would have known how much my encouragement meant to her. Perhaps someone feels the same way about you but hasn't taken the time to write a letter. Or perhaps it's time for you to think about someone who needs to receive a letter like this from you!

I was also surprised and touched recently when Steve Schanwald, executive vice president of business operations for the Chicago Bulls, sent me a copy of a letter of encouragement I wrote to him over twenty-five years ago. Along with my own letter, Steve sent me this note:

> You won't remember this, but you were very kind to a young kid, many years ago, just starting out in life. I was cleaning the attic the

other day and came across your letter. I don't think there is anything more rewarding in our profession than helping young people climb the ladder of success. You were "Big Time," and I wasn't, but you treated me like I was. Thanks for that.

### Be Careful Who You Follow

*I have realized that because of what I do, people want to be like me, so I try to spend every day of my life becoming more like Jesus.*
—Kurt Warner<br>Quarterback, St. Louis Rams

Did you ever play Follow-the-Leader when you were a kid? Remember that game where you had to follow another boy or girl as they walked, hopped, skipped, jumped, and ran around the neighborhood? If you didn't copy the leader's movements perfectly, you were "out." If you were the last one left who was still following, you got to be the new leader, and it was your turn to put the other kids through their paces.

I remember that I hated it when one boy became the leader. He was difficult to follow. The worst part was that he did things that seemed kind of dangerous and dumb. He climbed walls, he jumped out of trees, he led us into places we didn't really want to be, like spooky backyards with "Beware of Dog" signs.

Like I said, I didn't like it very much, but I followed him anyway. After all, he was the leader and it was my duty to follow. I never stopped to think that I didn't have to play the game his way.

In a certain sense, nobody has ever quit playing that game. We're all following leaders of some sort. We follow our bosses at work. We follow our pastors and elders at church. We follow the example of our neighbors, who just bought that shiny new SUV. We follow the leaders of our government, political party, professional organization, or labor union.

In all of these situations, it is important to be careful whom we follow. That's why the apostle Paul wrote these words to the church at Corinth: "Follow my example, as I follow the example of Christ" (1 Corinthians 11:1).

We're all leaders in some ways, and we're all followers in some ways. If we want to be effective leaders, we need to follow and learn from the right people. My boss, Rich DeVos, is a great leader, but he also knows how to be a follower. Recently I was talking with a gentleman who serves on a board with DeVos, and he told me, "If the organization Rich is working with has good leadership, he's perfectly willing to follow. He's willing to be the leader if that's necessary, but he doesn't have to be the leader."

I owe much of my success to people like DeVos, R. E. Littlejohn, Bill Veeck, Bob Carpenter, Chuck Hall—who was my financial advisor for years—and longtime NBA executive Norm Sonju. Today I also consider my close friend Jay Strack to be a mentor. Even though he's quite a bit younger than I am, I have learned so much from his wisdom and knowledge.

A couple of years ago, after I spoke at the Rotary Club in Windermere, Florida, a man named George Bailey came up to me, shook my hand, and said, "You were very fortunate to have mentors like Bill Veeck, Rich DeVos, and Mr. Littlejohn."

I smiled and agreed. "I sure was."

"And now," he said, "you're one of them."

His comment touched me and made me think. If I am able to influence other people's lives in a positive way, it's only because people like Mr. Littlejohn and Rich DeVos have influenced my life in a positive way. It is so important to follow the right people as you go through life.

This is true no matter how old you are, but it is especially important if you're just starting out in your career. You can gain so much by seeking out the wisdom of those who have walked the path you're walking now. That's what I did when I was starting out in the sports business, and it was a tremendous help to me. Now don't sit around and wait for mentors to seek you out. Be proactive! It's worth it!

That reminds me of what Paul says in 2 Timothy 2:2: "And the things you have heard me say in the presence of many witnesses entrust to reliable men who will also be qualified to teach others." Although Paul doesn't say so, what he's talking about here is a chain reaction. In other words, "Entrust to reliable men who will also be qualified to teach others...who will be able to teach others...who will be able to teach others...and so on down through history." You never can tell where your influence for good—or bad—will end. It may last for hundreds or thousands of years!

Buck O'Neil, a hero of the old Negro Leagues, is ninety-one years old. He finished his baseball career before blacks were permitted to play in the major leagues. Nevertheless, he is not the least bit bitter or resentful. When I had a chance to talk with him about his amazing career, he said he believes that every human being has been born at exactly the right time—and that everything we have has been passed down to us from the previous generation. Our job, given by God, is to pass the benefit of our wisdom and experience on to those who will come after us.

S. Truett Cathy, founder of Chick Fil-A, has said, "If you wish to enrich days, plant flowers. If you wish to enrich years, plant trees. If you wish to enrich eternity, plant ideals in the lives of others."

Consider the history of two families who lived in New York for generations. The first family can trace its roots back to a godly man, a minister named Jonathan Edwards. Down through the generations this family produced more than one hundred attorneys, thirty judges, sixty physicians, one hundred clergymen, fourteen college presidents, and about sixty authors. Members of this family have served on boards of directors of hospitals, banks, and important industries throughout the United States.

The other family, the Jukes family, sprang from a man who refused to work or learn a trade and had no education. Of his 1,200 descendants, 130 spent time in prison, including 7 who were convicted of murder. Another 440 were ruined by alcoholism or drug addiction, and 310 spent their days living off the state or the generosity of others. It is reported that only 12 of these 1,200 people learned a trade, and 10 of these learned that trade in prison.

As I said earlier, you never know how far your influence will stretch.

New York City Mayor Rudy Guliani, who became a national hero in the aftermath of the September 11, 2001, attack on the World Trade Center, has written: "All leaders are influenced by those they admire. Reading about them and studying their traits inevitably allows an inspiring leader to develop his own leadership traits."

Of course, some people choose to follow the wrong leaders. I saw in the paper recently that Susan Atkins has again been denied parole by the State of California. Atkins has been in prison since the late 1960s. She seems to be a gentle, sweet woman—a Christian since the early 1970s—who is nearly sixty years old. She is serving a life term because in the 1960s she chose to follow a fellow by the name of Charles Manson. She took part in a brutal murder spree because he told her to. When you look at Susan Atkins today, you can't help but wonder how she ever could have hurt anyone—let alone kill them.

When you are following the wrong leaders, you are going to wind up at the wrong destination. That's just the way it is! For example, nearly sixty years after World War II came to an end, I still have a hard time understanding how a country like Germany—with such a proud history—could have fallen into the hands of a maniac like Adolf Hitler! This is the country that produced great composers, writers, and thinkers like Ludwing van Beethoven, Johann Sebastian Bach, Johannes Brahms, Johann Pachelbel, Paul Tillich, Karl Barth, Herman Hesse, Immanuel Kant, Albert Einstein, Albert Schweitzer, Johann Gutenberg, and many more. Yet this proud, cultured nation produced one of the most barbaric political systems our world has ever seen.

How could such savagery spring out of such intellect? The German people chose to follow the wrong leader. Who you follow is so important. As Denver Broncos football Coach Mike Shanahan has said, "It's easy to become a winner if you're simply willing to learn from those who have been winners themselves."

### Every Action Carries a Message

*Nearly 90 percent of how people learn is visual. It's what they see...People need to see a sermon, more than hear it, to really embrace it. A leader's credibility and his right to be followed are based on his life as much as his lip.*
*—John Maxwell*

Edwin Hubbel Chapin said, "Every action of our lives touches a cord that will vibrate in eternity." Similarly, when someone asked Dr. Albert Schweitzer how children learn, he answered: "First, by example. Second, by example. And third, by example."

Francis of Assisi once invited a young monk to go with him into a neighboring village to preach. Francis had already gained a widespread reputation as a great man of God, so the monk accepted his invitation with enthusiasm. The two of them traveled into the town, where they spent the day tending to the needs of the poor and suffering. All day long the young monk waited for Francis to set up a place where they could preach; but before that ever happened, the sun started to set, and it was time for the two men to head back home.

On their way out of town, the monk told Francis that he was confused and disappointed. "I thought we were going to preach," he said.

Francis responded gently, "My son, we did preach. We were preaching while we were walking. We were watched by many, and our behavior was closely observed. It is of no use to walk anywhere to preach unless we preach everywhere as we walk." On another occasion St. Francis advised his followers, "Preach the Gospel at all times. Use words if necessary."

Pastor Andy Stanley says, "To gain and maintain influence, you must have moral authority...Without moral authority your influence will be limited and short-lived." What is moral authority? Stanley says it is, "the credibility you earn by walking your talk. It is the relationship other people see between what you say and what you do, between what you claim to be and what you are. A person with moral authority is beyond reproach. That is, when you look for a discrepancy between what he says he believes and what he does, you come up empty."

Tom Landry, the highly successful head coach of the Dallas Cowboys for so many years, was a man like that. Roger Staubach, who quarterbacked the Cowboys for many years under Landry, said, "Tom Landry's faith and deeds went hand-in-hand. That's why he was so beloved. He lived his faith every day in so many ways."

Dan Reeves, who also played for Landry and is now the head coach of the Atlanta Falcons, remembers, "Coach Landry wasn't one to preach to you every day. He led his life. He walked the talk." A smile spreads across Reeves' face as he says, "The things he talked about and showed in his life have helped me become a better person. Hopefully I can have the influence on half as many people as Coach Landry influenced in his life."

Long ago Tom Landry had made a decision we all must make. We have to decide if we want to impress people or influence them. Landry decided that he wanted to influence them for good, and in order to do that he had to get close enough for them to see his good example.

Incidentally, when I had the thrill of interviewing Tom Landry for my radio show a few years ago, he told me that he had always admired Paul Brown, the long-time coach of the Cleveland Browns. In fact, Landry said that he had built his entire career on the things he had learned from Brown. On the sidelines, he even wore a hat just like the one Brown had always worn. There's that thing called "influence" again.

Author Rick Warren puts it like this, "You can impress people from a distance, but you must get close to influence them." He goes on to say that you'll have to get so close, in fact, that they will be able to see your flaws—but that's okay. Warren says, "The most essential quality for leadership is not perfection but credibility. People must be able to trust you."

John Maxwell adds, "People are changed not by coercion or intimidation but by example."

**Do Your Best All the Time**

*We cannot live through a single day without making an impact on the world around us. We all have free choice...what sort of difference do we want to make? Do we want to make the world a better place. Or not?*

—Jane Goodall

Coach Bob Valvano grew up in a basketball family and spent six weeks every summer at a basketball camp run by his father. His older brother Jim went on to lead North Carolina State University to a national championship. As Bob tells it, one day at noon he and some of his friends were horsing around on one of the courts prior to a shooting contest. On the way home after the contest Jim said, "You didn't shoot very well today, did you?"

Bob was surprised. "What are you talking about? I didn't win, but I wasn't bad."

Jim replied, "I'm not talking about the contest it-self. During lunch you missed eight shots in a row."

Bob protested that he and his friends were just goofing around, and that it really didn't matter that he had missed all those shots. Jim shook his head. He had been watching with a prominent college basketball coach, who said, "Your brother isn't a bad player, but he doesn't shoot real well, does he?"

After passing along that sobering bit of informa-tion, Jim went on to give this advice: "Remember this. Every time you step between the lines, someone will be watching you. They don't know if you're goofing around or sick or tired or hurt. All they know is what they see. When you are between those lines assume somebody important is out there watching and ask yourself, 'What are they thinking of how I'm doing? Today. Right now.'"

You never know when an action you take will make a lasting impression on someone. So it is terribly im-portant to make sure that all of your actions are prop-er and good. I don't think anybody's ever said it better than J. R. Miller in his book, *The Building of Character*. "There have been meetings of only a moment that have left impressions for life, for eternity. No one can un-derstand that mysterious thing we call influence...yet every one of us continually exerts influence; either to heal, to bless, to leave marks of beauty; or to wound, to hurt, to poison, to stain other lives."

General Robert E. Lee, Commander-in-Chief of Confederate forces during the Civil War, was a deeply religious man, who sought always to lead by example. Lee believed that slavery was immoral and had freed his own family's slaves, but he had reluctantly joined the South to defend against what he saw was a war of aggression by the North.

One day after the war was over, Lee went out for a walk on a snowy day, followed by his eight-year old son, Custis. At one point the general turned around to see how his son was making his way through the deepening snowdrifts. He was surprised to see that Custis was carefully imitating his father, taking giant steps so that his own feet would land in the boot tracks his father had made in the snow. Lee was deeply moved by this and later told a friend, "When I saw this, I said to myself, 'It behooves me to walk very straight when this fellow is already following my tracks.'"

Every parent should know what Robert E. Lee came to understand on that snowy afternoon. Your children want to follow in your path. They are watching you at all times, learning from the things you do. Therefore, it behooves you to walk carefully. The late author James Baldwin said, "Children have never been very good at listening to their elders, but they have never failed to imitate them."

A woman in Virginia was watching her young son playing with a football in the backyard. He pretended to run for a touchdown. Then he dropped to his knees for a quick prayer of thanks, just as he had seen many of his NFL heroes doing. "I wonder," his mother said, "if these NFL players have any idea how much influence they have on some kids' lives."

My youngest son, Alan, is a seventeen-year-old junior at a small Christian High School. He's a great kid, but he can't seem to stay out of trouble. Just about every other day we get another phone call from the school, telling us about something he's done. I've told him over and over again, "Alan, I want you to be a leader."

His response is, "I don't want to be a leader." (He knows that leaders can't goof off.) Yet, a couple of weeks ago he came home with some exciting news. His coach has named him captain of the school basketball team.

I said, "Alan, that's awesome. And do you know what it means?"

He thought for a moment and then said, "I'm a *leader*?" And when he said the word "leader," his voice went up about an octave. As Alan is finding out, leadership is sometimes thrust upon us. And when that happens, it's time to step up the plate and meet the challenge. Remember:

> My life shall touch a dozen lives
> Before this day is done,
> Leave countless marks for good or ill
> Ere sets the evening sun.
> This is the wish I always wish,
> The prayer I always pray,
> Lord may my life help other lives
> It touches by the way.

These are some very good words to live by!

## Be Willing to Pay the Price

*I have found that the most effective way to bring out the best in people on my team is to lead by example. The problem? You have to pay a price to be that kind of leader. You often have to be the first to work and the last to leave. You must be one of the hardest, most conscientious workers, producing the best quality product possible.*

–Joe Gibbs, Former Coach
Washington Redskins

It's not always easy to be a good example. It can require a lot of very hard work, but in the long run it is well worth it. If more people were willing to pay that price, this country never would have found itself in the crisis of character that faces us today.

Writer Greg Morris says, "We cannot lead others any further than we have gone ourselves. We cannot expect our followers to exhibit a commitment to excellence, honesty, integrity, or other traits unless they have first been demonstrated in our lives."

Colin Powell has said, "You can issue all the memos and give all the motivational speeches you want, but if the rest of the people in your organization don't see you putting forth your very best effort every single day, they won't either."

Legendary football coach Vince Lombardi was a smoker, but when a mother wrote to him, expressing her concern about the example he was setting for children, he quit. It wasn't easy, but he was willing to pay the price to be a good influence.

When a woman approached Mahatma Gandhi and asked if he would please tell her son that it wasn't healthy to eat candy, the great leader asked her to bring her son back in two weeks. She agreed. When she came back two weeks later, she asked the great spiritual leader why he couldn't have talked to her son the first time. "Because I was still eating sweets then myself," he said. Of course, giving up candy was only one of the many ways he was willing to expend the effort to be a good influence.

I will never forget how Julius Erving—the great Dr. J—appeared at a basketball clinic in upstate New York for me on a hot, humid, summer afternoon at the height of his playing days in the late 1970s. Later on, I discovered that he had flown home from another clinic in Colorado the night before, grabbed a couple of hours sleep, and then headed north to my clinic at Schroon Lake.

There were more than one thousand kids at that clinic, which took place outdoors on a broiling hot day. Nevertheless, Dr. J threw himself into it with all his might. He had time for everyone, was patient and kind, and left memories those kids would never forget. The man was so tired he was about to drop, but he didn't let it show.

Dr. J didn't have to come to my clinic. He didn't really have anything to gain from it because he did it for free, as a favor to me. He already had enough

money, fame, and power. He didn't have to do anything he didn't want to do. But he did it for the kids.
He was willing to pay the price. And who knows? On
that stifling, hot, summer's day in upstate New York,
Dr. J just might have changed the world!

Just like you might have changed the world by
what you did today. Or what you do tomorrow. Or the
day after tomorrow.

# CHAPTER TWELVE

# HAVE COURAGE

*Be strong and courageous.*
—Joshua 1:9

On September 11, 2001, 343 firefighters died in the aftermath of the terrorist attack on the World Trade Center in New York City. Entire companies were wiped out in an effort to save lives. To help put the horrible loss in perspective, consider the fact that the previous biggest loss for the New York City Fire Department occurred in 1966, when twelve men died fighting a fire in Manhattan.

Can you imagine the courage that sent those firefighters rushing into that inferno? I can't. As they ran into the buildings, thousands of other people were running out of them, trying to escape with their lives.

David Frank, a salesman who managed to make it out safely from his office on the seventy-eighth floor, says that as he was hurrying down the stairs, he passed a group of firefighters heading up. "They were perspiring profusely," he said. "They were exhausted, and they had to go all the way to the nineties—straight into hell."

Frank remembers that he and the others who were heading down the stairs broke into applause as the firefighters rushed past them. They couldn't have known for sure that those firefighters were rushing to their deaths. Yet that's exactly where they were headed.

I am reminded of Christ's words, "Greater love has no one than this, that he lay down his life for his friends" (John 15:13). From now on, whenever I hear the word "courage," I will remember the firefighters who gave their lives on September 11.

I will also remember that courage has other faces as well.

Winston Churchill said, "Courage is rightly esteemed the first of human qualities, because it is the quality which guarantees all others." Courageous people stand up for what is right, no matter what other people may think or say. They do not check to see which way the wind is blowing before they act. They don't rely on public opinion polls. They don't give in to peer pressure. They realize that life itself is a risk, and they're willing to take that risk.

Andrew Jackson said, "One man with courage makes a majority." For me, that just about sums it up. Courageous people do what is right, no matter what other people may think or say. They do not check to see which way the wind is blowing before they act. They don't rely on public opinion polls. They don't give in to peer pressure. They realize that life itself is a risk, and they're willing to take that risk.

You may not consider yourself to be a person of courage, but you are. If you stop to think about it, you'll see that it requires a great deal of courage just to get out of bed in the morning and face the day. If you were not a person of courage, you'd never be able to ride in a car. After all, cars are involved in 20 percent of all fatal accidents.

You'd never be able to travel by air, rail, or water, because those types of transportation are involved in another 16 percent of fatal accidents. You couldn't cross the street, because 15 percent of all accidents happen on the street. And you certainly couldn't stay home, because 17 percent of all accidents happen there!

If you didn't have courage, you couldn't do anything at all. Not even exist! But as David Viscott has written:

If you cannot risk, you cannot grow.
If you cannot grow, you cannot become your best.
If you cannot become your best, you cannot be happy.
If you cannot be happy, what else matters?

If we turn around those risks that we just talked about and look at them in another way, we'll discover that in an average year:

- You have a 1 in 115 chance of dying of natural causes.

- You have a 1 in 2,900 chance of losing your life in an automobile accident.

- Chances are 1 in 80,000 that you will die of complications from surgery.
- Odds are 250,000 to 1 against your dying in an airplane crash.
- There is a 1 in 1 million chance that you will lose your life in a bathtub accident!

Statistically, you are more likely to be kicked to death by a donkey than die in a plane crash. You are eight times more likely to die playing a sport than you are from being involved in a car crash, even if you drive on a daily basis. And you are three times more likely to be struck by lightning than to win the lottery, even though I don't advise anyone to play the lottery.

Perhaps you feel like the comedian who said, "I want to die quietly, in my sleep, like my grandfather. Not screaming like the other people in his car." Or maybe you're like Woody Allen, who said, "I'm not afraid of dying. I just don't want to be there when it happens."

Why am I talking about death so much? Because most of us think of death as the worst thing that can happen. But death should hold no fear for the Christian. It doesn't even exist. One moment you're here, the next you're in Paradise with the Lord. There is nothing at all to be afraid of. And once we understand that, we can be courageous in the face of lesser threats.

I believe there are at least five important areas where we can change ourselves and our world by demonstrating courage.

- Have the courage to stand up for what's right.

- Have the courage to get involved.

- Have the courage to lead an ethical life.

- Remember that courage is contagious.

- Have the courage to take necessary risks.

## Have the Courage to Stand Up for What's Right

*Life shrinks or expands in proportion to one's courage.*

—Adlai Stevenson

For Jackie Robinson 1947 was the best of times and the worst of times. It was the best of times because that was the year he became the first black man to play major league baseball. It was the worst of times because he had not to endure unbelievable abuse from white opponents and white fans who did not want him to be there.

Years later Robinson admitted that he was often tempted to retaliate in kind. But whenever that happened, he thought of his wife and his little boy. He also thought of all the good black players who were counting on him to open doors for them—and who would never get a chance if he didn't handle the opportunity correctly.

On April 22 the Philadelphia Phillies came to play the Dodgers in Brooklyn, and manager Ben Chapman was on Robinson's back all day. "Hey snowflake!" "When did they let you out of the jungle." "We don't need no niggers down here." And worse.

Robinson silently endured the torrent of abuse. Then, in the eighth inning, he singled up the middle, stole second, moved to third on a wild throw, and scored on another single by Gene Hermanski. The Dodgers won 1-0.

Two weeks later, the Dodgers were in Philadelphia. This time Chapman started yelling at their shortstop, Pee Wee Reese, who was from the South—Louisville, Kentucky, to be exact. "Hey, Reese!" he shouted. "How you like playing with a nigger?"

When Pee Wee ignored him, Chapman shouted the question again and again. Finally, Reese stopped picking up ground balls and jogged over to Robinson at first base. Then, staring into the Philadelphia dugout, he put his arm around Jackie Robinson's shoulders. Dodger teammate, Gene Hermanski, remembers, "Pee Wee didn't say a word, but Chapman had his answer."

I wonder what I would have done if I had been Jackie Robinson. Or how I would have responded to Ben Chapman if I had been Pee Wee Reese. Would I have been so quick to go over and put my arm around my black teammate? I certainly hope so. More than that, I hope I will have the courage to stand up for the right thing today, even in the face of terrible opposition and hostility, just like firemen rushing through an inferno and a little girl named Ruby Bridge.

I grew up in a segregated society. When I attended high school in Wilmington, Delaware, in the late 1950s, there were no black students at my school. In 1956 my dad, Jim, who had grown up in the South—North

Carolina, to be exact—worked with Bob Carpenter of the Philadelphia Phillies to organize the first Delaware high school all-star football game.

Two black players from Howard High, Joe Peters and Alvin Hall, made the northern team, but the prep school where the team was practicing would not let them stay in its dorms. My dad said, "Well, then they'll stay at our house." That's what they did. I've never forgotten the courageous stand my dad took that year, nor have I forgotten the courage of those two young football players who held their heads high and showed no bitterness in the face of wrong treatment.

That brings to mind another occasion when I had an even more personal encounter with courage in the face of blatant racism. In 1962 I played for the Phillies' farm team in the Florida State League, which was totally segregated. Black players stayed at one hotel; white players at another. After our last game of the season, our first baseman, Fred Mason, who was black and from Wilmington, asked if we could drive home together. I said, "Sure." I was happy for the company.

About 2 a.m. we reached Jacksonville, where we stopped for gas. I went into the restroom, and when I came out a big, burly guy with a crowbar in his hand—I think he was the station owner—was chasing Fred toward my car. His eyes were bulging out of their sockets, the veins on his forehead were standing out, and he was screaming a torrent of obscenities in Fred's direction—simply because Fred was black.

Thankfully we beat the guy to the car, hopped in, and peeled rubber out of there. For a long time we were too shaken to speak, and then Fred said, "Well, some of my friends would have torn that place apart." We didn't stop again until we reached Wilmington, but I've never forgotten Fred Mason's example of quiet courage.

Another great example of courage was the Apostles themselves. They would not deny the truth that God sent His Son into the world to bring us eternal life. And here is what it cost them:

**James** was beheaded in 36 AD, the first of the twelve to die.

**Thomas** was killed by a dart, while on a missionary trip to India.

**Simon** the Zealot was crucified, as were **Bartholomew** and **Andrew**.

**Matthew** was run through with a spear.

**James** the Less was thrown to his death from the top of a temple.

**Peter** was crucified upside down.

And so it went until every one of the twelve—with one exception—died a painful martyr's death. The only one who lived to old age was John, who died in exile on the Island of Patmos. If people oppose us because we stand for what is right, we are in some very, very good company.

Alan Hobson has some good words about courage. "Courage is not only the ability to risk your life; it is the ability to stand fast when everything else around you is falling apart, to remain calm when everyone else around you is losing their heads. In the simplest sense it is getting up every day to make a better life for yourself, or starting a new job, or re-marrying, or moving to a new city."

He goes on: "If you are faced with a decision, no matter how small, ask yourself if you are acting out of courage or out of fear. If you are acting out of fear, the result will be predictable. If you are acting out of courage, success could be within your grasp."

### Have the Courage to Get Involved

*Courage is not the absence of fear. It is*
*the making of action in spite of fear; the moving*
*out against the resistance engendered by fear*
*into the unknown and into the future.*

—M. Scott Peck
Writer/Psychologist

"I don't want to get involved." Have you ever heard someone say that? Have you ever said it yourself? That's understandable, because there are plenty of reasons not to get involved, especially in this dangerous time.

If you see a man beating his wife or girlfriend, you might not want to get involved because he could pull out a gun and shoot you. If you see a traffic accident, you might not want to get involved because someone could blame you for their injuries and sue you. And if you witness a crime of some sort, you might not get involved because it will take so much of your time. No wonder some people think it's better just to look straight ahead and keep their blinders on.

But not getting involved leads to anarchy, terror, and scandal.

On the night of March 13, 1964, a young woman named Kitty Genovese was stabbed to death in Queens, New York, in front of many of her neighbors, none of whom called the police. When she first cried out for help, several people looked out from their upper floor apartments. One man even shouted for the killer to leave her alone, but then he shut his window and went back to bed.

After she was killed, Kitty's body lay in the street for nearly three hours before anyone called the police. During their investigation of the murder, authorities determined that thirty-eight people had seen the fatal attack. Not one of them was willing to do anything about it. This is the price we pay for not being willing to get involved.

Edmund Burke said, "The only thing necessary for the triumph of evil is for good men to do nothing." Moreover, God calls us to be involved in life. He tells us to "Carry each other's burdens" (Galatians 6:2). We can't do that if we don't have the courage to become involved with each other. He also tells us to meet the needs of those who are hungry and thirsty, to clothe

the naked, to be hospitable to strangers, to look after the sick, and to visit those who are in prison. (See Matthew 25:34-40.) You certainly can't do any of these things if you don't have the courage to get involved.

How can we be the light of the world or salt of the earth if we're holed up at home watching television? You may say, "That may be true, but how do you get the courage you need to get involved in life?"

The first way is to pray, for as someone has said, "Courage is fear that has said its prayers." The second way is to understand that, as Ambrose Redmoon said, "Courage is not the absence of fear, but rather, the judgment that something is more important than fear." General Omar Bradley put it like this: "Bravery is the capacity to perform properly even when scared half-to-death."

Theodore Roosevelt, who had a well-deserved reputation as a rough-and-ready adventurer, once said that he went through a time in which, "there were all kinds of things of which I was afraid...but by acting as if I were not afraid, I gradually ceased to be afraid. Most men can have the same experience if they choose." Ralph Waldo Emerson put the same thought in a slightly different way: "Do the thing you fear, and the death of fear is certain." Believe me—you can make a tremendous difference in this world, if you are willing to do it.

I mentioned earlier that Mary Kay Ash's accountants thought she was making a huge mistake when she decided to launch her line of cosmetics. Today just about everyone is familiar with her organization and its famous fleet of pink Cadillacs. When someone asked Mary Kay why more people didn't fulfill their potential, she said, "Fear is what holds people back, fear of rejection, of not succeeding, of losing whatever money you have. All the fears that we have as human beings keep us from reaching our potential. If there's one equal factor where many women are concerned, it's a lack of self-confidence."

Are you afraid to step out and get involved in life? If so, you should know that:

- 60 percent of people's fears are totally unwarranted.

- 20 percent of the things we fear are already in the past, and there's nothing we can do to change them.

- 10 percent of our fears are so small that they wouldn't really affect our lives.

- Only 4 to 5 percent of our fears are real and justifiable, and half of these are beyond our ability to control.

So why allow fear to hold us back?

### Have the Courage to Lead an Ethical Life

*Fear God, and you need not be afraid of anyone else.*
                                    —Woodrow Wilson

As you know, Ruth and I have nineteen children. Because of this, we have a rule: No hanging around home after high school. Once you have that diploma, you're either going to college, into the military, or getting a job.

In May 1999 Thomas and Stephen, our adopted twins from South Korea, graduated from high school. Stephen enrolled immediately for summer classes at Florida State University in Tallahassee. We loaded his belongings into my car and made the four-hour drive north from Orlando. I got him settled in his dorm room, had dinner with him, and then it was time for me to make the drive back home. I hugged him, told him I loved him, and then drove away with a huge lump in my throat.

As I looked in the rearview mirror I saw him waving goodbye. I began to pray, "Lord, he's only seventeen, but please give him courage and wisdom beyond his years. Help him to stand up for what he knows is right." I watched him head back toward the dorm and thought about how many times we all reach an important crossroads in life—and how important it is, when we do, to stand up for the things we believe in.

When I think of people who let fear keep them from living an ethical life, the first person who comes to mind is Pontius Pilate, the man who allowed Jesus to be crucified. He tried every non-courageous thing he could think of to keep Jesus alive. First, he told Jesus' accusers that he found no fault in the man. When that didn't work, he had Jesus beaten in hopes that would satisfy their anger.

When that didn't help, he offered them the choice of setting one man free—Jesus or a common criminal named Barabbas. No doubt he was shocked when the crowd chose Barabbas. Even so, he gave in to them. To show that he wouldn't accept responsibility for Jesus' death, he washed his hands in front of the crowd before handing Jesus over to be crucified.

The only thing Pilate didn't do was the one thing that could have prevented Jesus' execution. He could have pronounced a verdict of not guilty and set Him free. But he wouldn't do that because he was afraid of the mob.

Of course, we know that it was God's will for Jesus to die for our sins, but one of the ways He brought this about was through Pontius Pilate's fear of an angry mob. I think we can all sympathize to some degree with Pilate. After all, every one of us knows how difficult it can be to stand up for what's right when the rest of the world seems to be on the side of wrong.

Truthfully, I can't remember another time when unethical behavior was as prevalent and as accepted as it is today. Everywhere I go I see teenagers who aren't gang-bangers trying to look like gang-bangers. They dress like them, talk like them, and act like them because they think it's cool. Frankly, it's not cool.

God calls us to stand up for what is right and good, even when everyone around us wants to be bad. He calls us to be like those New York City firefighters, to run in the opposite direction from everyone else, because we're doing what we can to save our society. The Bible tells us, "Anyone, then, who knows the good he ought to do and doesn't do it, sins" (James 4:17).

The Chinese philosopher Confucius put a slightly different twist on it. He said, "To see what is right and not to do it is want of courage." Courage, like many of the other character traits we've discussed in this book, can be developed over time. If you practice being courageous during lesser trials, you'll develop a courage big enough to handle anything life throws at you.

Pastor/author Lloyd Ogilvie has a friend who was a trapeze artist when he was a young man. He told Ogilvie that the first time he fell during practice, he was scared half out of his mind. But over time, as he fell again and again, he became confident that the net below him was strong and reliable, and that he would not be hurt if he fell. He says that he actually learned to fall successfully and added, "Each fall makes you able to risk more."

Aristotle said, "Whatever we learn to do, we learn by actually doing it. Men come to be builders, for instance, by building; harp players by playing the harp. In the same way, by doing just acts we come to be just; by doing self-controlled acts we come to be self-controlled, and by doing brave acts we become brave." Here are a few areas where most of us can work on developing more courage.

- It takes courage to openly express your faith in God when you're living in a world that doubts Him.

- It takes courage to be optimistic about the future if you're surrounded by people who think it's cool to be pessimistic and cynical.

- It takes courage to be honest when nobody you know seems to think there's anything wrong with cheating.

- It takes courage to be faithful to your spouse in a world that glorifies sex and seems to think that monogamy is old-fashioned and square.

- If you're not married, it takes courage to stand up for personal purity.

- It takes courage to say no thanks when someone asks you if you want to hear a dirty joke.

- It takes courage to express your displeasure if someone makes a racist remark or tells a racist joke.

- It takes courage to ask someone to please stop using the Lord's name as a swear word.

- If you are a college or a high school student, it may take a great deal of courage to walk away from a party where people are drinking and smoking pot.

- It takes courage to refuse to gossip when you're in the lunchroom at work or having coffee with a neighbor.

- It takes courage to obey the rules when all your neighbors are cutting corners.

- It takes courage to express love in a world that is charged with anger and hate.

- It may even take courage to leave the office at a decent hour every evening so you can spend some time with your family.

All of these may not apply to you, but perhaps you can think of more areas where you definitely need to work on developing more courage. Remember that, as Florence Nightingale said, "Courage is...the universal virtue of all those who choose to do the right thing over the expedient thing. It is the common currency of all those who do what they are supposed to do in a time of conflict, crisis, and confusion."

I also urge you to do as Orison Swett Marden advises: "Don't wait for extraordinary opportunities. Seize common ones and make them great."

### Courage Is Contagious

*Courage is contagious. When a brave man takes*
*a stand, the spines of others are stiffened.*

—Billy Graham

In his book, *Man's Search for Meaning*, Psychiatrist Viktor Frankl writes about the horrors he endured as an inmate of a Nazi concentration camp during World War II. He says that for many men, a time came when they just gave up and decided to die. When that happened, hopelessness could be seen in their eyes, their actions, and their body language.

It's not surprising that this happened. Every day these men saw the bodies of fellow inmates being carried out of the camp. Those who weren't executed often died from a combination of disease, abuse, and hunger. Every man in those camps knew that the odds of surviving were not in his favor. However, even in the midst of such a horribly difficult situation, some men were able to maintain an attitude of hope and courage. They did this by remembering that life has a larger meaning, a meaning that extended far beyond the walls of any prison. They demonstrated a confidence that enabled them to survive and gave many of their fellow inmates the courage to keep going as well.

Thankfully, most of us will never know what it's like to be subjected to such inhumane treatment. But in whatever situation we find ourselves, we can demonstrate courage that will bring hope to others and enable them to be courageous too.

I heard about a college philosophy class in which the professor referred to himself as a "convinced atheist." He often mocked and ridiculed faith in God and was especially venomous toward anyone who believed in Jesus Christ. Most of his students sat in silence while he raved on. There was one young woman in the class—Audrey—who spoke up about her faith, but she seemed to be a lone voice crying in the wilderness.

One day, after a particularly heated exchange, the professor wanted to show Audrey just how ridiculous her faith was. He obviously felt that none of his other students would be "superstitious" enough to believe in God. He said sarcastically, "I'd like to find out how many of you share Audrey's point of view. If you believe in God, I want you to stand up right now."

Audrey stood up, but nobody else moved.

"Go ahead," the professor sneered. "Don't be shy. Stand up." He glanced around the room. "Well," he said smugly, "it looks like you're outnumbered."

At that moment, a young man on the other side of the room stood up.

"Well, Adam, this is a surprise," the professor said. "I never would have thought..." Before he could finish his sentence, two more students stood up. Then another...and another...until half the students were standing to express their faith.

You see, courage is contagious!

I mentioned earlier in this chapter that James was the first of the Apostles to be executed. According to legend, the man who was responsible for James' arrest was so impressed by the apostle's courage that he became a Christian during the trial. He made a public profession of his faith and wound up being executed alongside the man he had arrested.

For all intents and purposes, the American Civil Rights movement shifted into high gear on December 1, 1955. That was the day a black woman named Rosa Parks refused to give up her seat on city bus in Montgomery, Alabama. She was arrested and booked into the city jail. Her arrest sparked the courage of a twenty-six-year-old pastor named Martin Luther King Jr., who led a 381-day boycott of the Montgomery city bus system. King inspired millions of other people throughout the United States—black and white—and gave them the courage to stand up against the injustice of racial discrimination.

Rosa Parks changed America forever because courage truly is contagious.

### Have the Courage to Take Necessary Risks

*It is from numberless acts of courage
and belief that human history is shaped.*
—Robert F. Kennedy

You can't do much of anything without taking a risk. For instance, as someone has written,

To laugh is to risk appearing the fool.

To weep is to risk appearing sentimental.

To reach out to another is to risk involvement.

To express feelings is to risk exposing your true self.

To place your ideas, your dreams, before the crowd is to risk their loss.

To love is to risk not being loved in return.

To live is to risk dying; to hope is to risk despair.

To try is to risk failure, but risks must be taken;

Because the greatest hazard in life is to risk nothing.

The person who risks nothing, does nothing, has nothing, and is nothing.

They may avoid suffering and sorrow,

But they simply cannot learn, feel, change, grow, love or live.

Only a person who risks is free.

Eric Jensen says, "Sometimes the thing that will help you become a winner is not something you dread doing or don't want to do, but rather, something you are dying to do yet don't have the courage to try. Successful people are those who are willing, at some critical point, to take a risk."

Walt Disney, who was always one of my heroes, built a multi-billion dollar company on the strength of a big-eared cartoon rodent named Mickey. He said, "Courage is the main quality of leadership, in my opinion, no matter where it is exercised. Usually it implies some risk, especially in new undertakings, courage to initiate something and keep it going."

Do you ever think that you are not courageous?

Baloney!

Just look at the things you have done in your life that required tremendous courage: You learned to walk, even though you fell down over and over again. You learned how to ride a bike, even though you probably took a tumble or two. You overcame your fear of water and learned to swim. You got a driver's license, even though it can be pretty dangerous out there on the highway.

If you're married, you either accepted or extended a marriage proposal, either of which takes plenty of courage. And if you have children—*well, don't tell me* you're lacking in courage. In fact, if you've had the courage to do any or all of the above, there's really no limit to what you can do!

Playwright Neil Simon, certainly one of the most prolific and successful writers of our day, is familiar with the fear that can paralyze us and keep us from moving forward. He is living proof of the good things that can happen when we set those fears aside and do what we've always been afraid to do. He says, "Don't listen to those who say, 'It's not done that way.' Maybe it's not, but maybe you'll do it anyway...Most important, don't listen when the little voice of fear inside you rears its ugly head."

Let me close this discussion of courage by taking you back to August 1964, as Winston Churchill lay dying in London's King Edward VIII Hospital. Former President Dwight Eisenhower, who partnered with Churchill to end Nazi aggression during World War II, sat by his bedside, holding his hand.

No words were spoken as two great men of the twentieth century shared memories of the struggles they went through together. After about ten minutes, Churchill let go of Eisenhower's hand and slowly, painstakingly formed his famous "V" for victory sign. Eisenhower, fighting back tears, pulled his chair back, stood up, saluted, turned, and walked out of the room. Outside in the hall he told his aide: "I just said goodbye to Winston, but you never say farewell to courage."

# CHAPTER THIRTEEN

# HAVE FAITH IN GOD

*Faith is to believe what you do not see;*
*the reward for this faith is to see what you believe.*

—Saint Augustine

I recently talked to a woman in her late sixties who is going through a health crisis. When we spoke she seemed relaxed and happy in spite of everything. "You don't seem very worried about this," I told her.

She laughed and replied, "I'm not." Then she explained why. "There have been so many times in my life when I had a problem that was too big for me to handle. Every time I said, 'God, I can't do this, so You'll have to take care of it. And every time He did. I've learned that I can trust Him in every situation."

This woman has discovered the reality of what I call "the faith phenomenon." Once you surrender control of your life to God, you learn that you can trust Him in all situations. It's vitally important for us all to remember, especially during these difficult days, that God is still in control of the universe. As the old song says, "He's got the whole world in His hands." Everything is going according to His plan. I love this quote from C. S. Lewis: "I believe in Christianity as I believe in the sunrise; not because I can see it, but because by it I can see everything else."

Faith in God is, by far, the primary means of coming safely through times of struggle and scandal. It is the only thing we can hold onto when the bad guys seem to be winning. Faith gives us the assurance that justice and truth will prevail in the end. It was faith that enabled Martin Luther King Jr. to endure beatings, death threats, and constant verbal abuse to continue his fight for Civil Rights. It was faith that helped Boris Yeltsin stand up against the communist regime that had held the Russian people captive for over seventy years. And ultimately, it will be faith at work in the hearts and lives of the American people that will help us overcome the difficult times we're facing.

Like nearly everything else we have discussed in this book, faith can be—and must be—strengthened with practice. Dr. Bill Bright, founder of Campus Crusade for Christ, says, "Faith is like a muscle; it grows with exercise, and the more we know of the trustworthiness and faithfulness of God...His grace, love, power, and wisdom...the more we can trust Him."

Tim Salmon, the elder statesman for the 2002 World Champion California Angels, says this about his faith in Christ: "I'm thankful that I had the opportunity to have my eyes opened and be enlightened as to the joy that is around me and that maybe I take for granted. I've had to persevere in my life, but it was always applied to baseball. For the first time in my life, I had to persevere in something much more important than baseball. That's what this whole spiritual journey is about—growing in our faith and being more Christlike every day." I know exactly what Tim Salmon is talking about, and I hope you do too.

As I work on this book today, I picture myself having a one-on-one conversation with you. Right now I feel certain that I am talking to someone who has surrendered her life to Christ. If not, I urge you to go back to Chapter Two and reconsider the prayer of salvation I included there. Believe me, it is an incredible joy to have a personal relationship with the One who created the entire universe. What a relief it is to be able to relax and know that God is in control of everything!

If you have not accepted Christ as your Lord and Savior, please don't let this opportunity pass you by. He is the anchor that will keep you safe during any season of scandal, disappointment, or grief. Listen to these words from St. Louis Cardinals' slugger J. D. Drew. "The plan of salvation is so simple, but many people miss it because they think they can work their way to heaven. That's what I did. I abided by the law and did the things it said, but the simplest thing to do is just to ask God to forgive you and accept His Son, Jesus Christ, as your Savior."

Following are some things I have discovered about faith during my own travels through the storms of life.

## Faith Brings Thrills

*It's pretty amazing and awesome that you*
*can have a relationship with the God*
*who created the rivers and the trees.*
—Shannon Dunn-Downing
Olympic Snowboarder

How did we ever get the idea that faith in God is connected to hard-backed pews, boring sermons, and dirge-like music? It is incredible to me that anyone could come into the presence of the Creator of the Universe and be bored. God isn't some white-bearded grandfather who likes to tell boring stories about the good old days. There is absolutely nothing about Him to bring on a yawn or cause your eyelids to start drooping.

Author Calvin Miller says, "Indeed, there may be only one sin for those who believe in Christ. It is the sin of knowing Christ but not holding His acquaintance special." There is nothing on earth that can begin to compare with a one-on-one relationship with God. Nothing!

In 2002 Arizona Diamondbacks pitcher Randy Johnson won a record fifth Cy Young Award. Was that the greatest thrill of his life? Here's what the six-foot, ten-inch fast-baller had to say: "The greatest feeling I get playing baseball right now is knowing that I can go out every fifth day and be a warrior for the Lord. I can go out behind the mound and crouch down and say my prayer, and then be a very aggressive, warrior-like pitcher, glorifying Him in that sense."

Tony Dungy, head coach of the Indianapolis Colts, says he has had many great moments on the football field, but nothing to compare with the excitement of a relationship with Christ. "The thrill of winning a Super Bowl is temporary," he said. "Receiving Christ counts for eternity."

Here's more from "Neon" Deion Sanders, the only person ever to play in both the Super Bowl and the World Series: "Before I found Christ, I had all the material comforts and all the money and all the fame and popularity, but I had no peace." Now he says, "No touchdown, no homerun, no stolen base, no tackle, no interception could compare to me leading someone to Jesus Christ. Nothing comes close."

Finally, this from Keith Smart, a former coach of the Cleveland Cavaliers, talking about one of the Bible's greatest verses—John 3:16: "One day when I was looking at John 3:16, it just jumped out. The beginning of my son's Social Security number is 316. I wore the number 316 on my shoes when I played. When I go and share, I talk about 3:16. I say, 'God so loved the world that He gave His only begotten Son, and whosoever believes in Him shall not perish but will have a brand new car, a brand new house, or money in the bank.' Some people think that because they have Christ in their life, those are the things they are going to receive from Him. No, we're talking about something that's going to be long-lasting and everlasting. Eternal life. That's a scripture that is very dear to me."

## Jesus Really Does Love You

*The story of Jesus is the story of a celebration—a story of love...Jesus embodies the promise of a God who will go to any length to win us back. Not the least of Jesus' accomplishments is that He made us, somehow, lovable to God.*

—Philip Yancey

As just about any seminary student will tell you, Karl Barth was a very deep thinker. Pastor/author Tony Evans remembers that Barth's thought processes were "so deep that we got headaches just trying to work through the course and grasp what he was saying."

Over half a century ago, when the brilliant theologian visited the United States, a young reporter asked him, "What is the greatest thought that has ever come into your mind?"

Without hesitation Karl Barth answered, "Jesus loves me, this I know, for the Bible tells me so." Karl Barth knew that this simple truth was the bottom line of all wisdom and knowledge. No matter how you say it—with small words and simple sentences or with huge words and complex sentences that seem to go on for pages, "Jesus loves me" is what it all comes down to.

Jesus loves you and me so much that He was willing to be born into a human body. That was the only way He could feel what you and I feel: The sting of a bee, the pain of a cut finger, the persistent toothache that keeps you up all night, the fever and chills that come with the flu. As the Son of God, Jesus knows everything, but it was only through being clothed in a human body that He came to experience first-hand what it feels like to be hungry, exhausted, cold, hot, ragged, and sweaty.

I like the way Calvin Miller puts it: "Let us remember that the whole idea of the Incarnation was that God became a man because it was the only way God could acquire a nervous system...Had He slipped in and out of the planet without pain, how would He ever have understood ours? His death makes Him our finest counselor when we face our own. Give me as my Savior no Greek god who frolics in indulgence, gluttony, and adultery. Give me, instead, a God who can hang in suffocating pain and tell me, even as He gasps, that life is never pointless."

## God Is in Control

*There's nothing that goes on where God says,*
*"Oops, I missed that one." Every circumstance*
*that happens in life, God has control of.*

—Matt Ware

Chances are good that you've never heard of Matt Ware, the young man who is quoted above. Chances are also good that you would have heard of him except for the terrible accident in 1998 that left him paralyzed. Matt was a standout high school basketball player with dreams of further success in the sport. Of course, those dreams died the day Matt was injured.

Matt doesn't understand why this happened to him, but he isn't bitter or angry about it because he knows for certain that his life is in God's hands. He has faith that God always sees the big picture, and he trusts that God is in control of everything. Does that mean God caused Matt Ware to become paralyzed? No! What it does mean is that God knew that it had to happen, and that He allowed it for some greater good that we are not yet able to see from our vantage point.

I know. Sometimes, it's difficult to believe that God is in control of everything that happens. But the Bible assures us that He is. There are times when we just have to accept that things are going to turn out right. As the Newsboys sing in their song, "Lord (I Don't Know),"

> Lord, we don't know where all this is going
>     or how it all works out.
> Lead me to peace that is past understanding,
>     a peace beyond all doubt.

The great preacher Charles Spurgeon wrote,

> God is too good to be unkind,
> He is too wise to be confused.
> If I cannot trace His hand,
> I can always trust His heart.

Wherever you are, right now, I want you to stop for a moment and think about the fact that God really is in control of your life and your situation. Let it sink in.

The gifted young pastor and author, Andy Stanley, says, "You don't know what God is up to behind the scenes of your life. You don't know how close you are to a breakthrough. It is no accident you are where you are, and it is not necessarily a problem that you are not where you assume you ought to be. God is very much in control."

He goes on to say that if you have made your relationship with God the top priority of your life, you can be sure that, "You are not wasting your time. You are not spinning your wheels. You are not wandering in the wilderness. If you are 'seeking first' His kingdom, where you are is where He positioned you."

Following the 2002 season, quarterback Rich Gannon of the Oakland Raiders was named the Most Valuable Player in the National Football League. Back in the mid-nineties, he was out of a job, and it looked like his brief career in the NFL was over. Even so, he never doubted that God was in control of his career and his life.

"I went from making a million dollars in 1993 to making zero dollars in 1994," he remembers. "There was a lot of uncertainty about whether I'd ever even play again. During that whole time, I never prayed to the Lord that He'd put me back in the National Football League...I just prayed for guidance and strength... that He would take control of my life and my situation and whatever He had in store for us."

Looking back as far as I can remember, the worst single moment the United States has ever experienced was the terrorist attacks on September 11, 2001. That was an unbelievably horrible day that we'll all remember as long as we live. Most of us would gladly give up everything we own if we could go back into the past and prevent that tragic loss of life from taking place. Nobody in his right mind could ever say that 9-11 was a good thing.

Even so, I can see how God was involved in that disaster, and how He brought good out of it. He brought us together as a nation. People stopped thinking of themselves as blacks, whites, Hispanics, or Asians; as Republicans, Democrats, or Independents; as Southerners, Northerners, Mid-Westerners, and so on. For a long time after the attacks, we considered ourselves to be only "Americans."

God used the attacks to turn many hearts toward Him. Many people learned that God is the only One we can turn to for comfort at a time like that. And He brought out the best in the American people. We gave sacrificially to help those who were injured, bereaved, and impacted in other ways by the attacks. We opened our pocketbooks and wallets and gave millions upon millions of dollars.

Bradley Hutcherson, vice-president of Texas Capital Bank in Dallas, sees some other ways God was in control on September 11. He was on four commercial flights giving terrified passengers the ability to stay calm. On one of those flights, He gave passengers the courage and strength to try to overcome the hijackers.

God acted to minimize the number of deaths. The four planes could have held one thousand passengers, but 266 people were on board. Of the fifty thousand people who normally worked in the World Trade Center's twin towers, thirty thousand were not in the buildings when the airplanes hit. Also, the plane that struck the Pentagon hit an area that was being remodeled. Hence, many of the offices in that wing were unoccupied. And finally, God held up the two 110-story towers of the World Trade Center long enough for two-thirds of the people inside to get out.

Even in the worst disasters, if you look closely enough, you will see God's hand at work.

**God Has a Plan for Your Life**

*God has a plan for all of us, but He*
*expects us to do our share of the work.*
—Minnie Pearl
Comedienne

During the Sermon on the Mount, Jesus said: "Look at the birds of the air; they do not sow or reap or store away in barns, and yet your heavenly Father feeds them. Are you not much more valuable than they?" (Matthew 6:26).

Not too long ago a construction crew that was building a road through a rural area came to a tree with a nest full of baby birds. The project superintendent marked the tree so that it wouldn't be cut down until the fledglings had flown from the nest.

A few weeks later, as work on the road progressed, the construction crew came back to that tree, and the superintendent was lifted up in a bucket truck so he could see if the nest was empty. It was, and he ordered his crew to cut the tree down. As it toppled to the ground, the empty nest bounced out of its branches. One of the workmen noticed that a piece of paper, with a few words written on it, was sticking out of it.

It was nothing, just part of the scraps of material that had been used to build the nest. But for some reason the workman bent down to take a closer look. He discovered that the paper was torn from a Sunday school book, and that it bore these words: "He careth for you."

What a lesson! God *does* care for the birds of the air, and He will care for you and me too. You are more valuable than sparrows and crows and starlings and wrens. You are more valuable than hawks and eagles and condors. God cherishes you and has a plan for your life.

What is His plan for you? The only Person who can answer that question is God. Dietrich Bonhoeffer said that one of the marks of a disciple of Christ is that he's not always sure where he's going. He's just following wherever Christ leads him. In my own life, I've often thought that God was going to take me in a certain direction, only to find out later on that He was actually preparing me for some other step He wanted me to take.

Will God call you to be a missionary to Africa? Perhaps. Will He ask you to go to seminary and prepare for full-time ministry? Maybe. But it's just as likely that

He wants you to stay right where you are and keep doing what you've been doing!

Chapter 19 of 1 Kings tells of a time when the great prophet Elijah was waiting for God to appear to him. "Then a great and powerful wind tore the mountains apart and shattered the rocks before the Lord, but the Lord was not in the wind. After the wind, there was an earthquake, but the Lord was not in the earthquake. After the earthquake came a fire, but the Lord was not in the fire. And after the fire came a gentle whisper" (1 Kings 19:11-12).

It was in the whisper that the prophet found the presence of God.

It isn't always in the great events and great acts that God can be experienced. Often He can be found in the routine events of daily life, especially when those events are offered up as service to Him by people who are seeking His will for their lives.

Pastor/author A. W. Tozer said, "Let us believe that God is in all our simple deeds and learn to find Him there. Let every man abide in the calling wherein he is called and his work will be as sacred as the work of the ministry." He goes on, "It is not what a man does that determines whether his work is sacred or secular...it is why he does it. Let a man sanctify the Lord God in his heart, and he can therefore do no common act."

If you do everything as "unto the Lord," whatever you do can be woven into the tapestry of God's plan for your life. Everything you experience can be used by Him for your good. Rose Kennedy, the matriarch of the Kennedy clan, suffered through many personal tragedies. Two children were killed in plane crashes, two more were assassinated, and one daughter, Rosemary, was born mentally disabled. At one point, perhaps understandably, Rose Kennedy grew very angry and bitter toward God.

One of the family's maids noticed this and told her, "Mrs. Kennedy, you need to get over this. The only way to do that is to make a manger in your heart and invite Jesus to come in." Such insolence added to Rose's anger, and she fired the maid on the spot.

That night Rose could not sleep. She twisted and tossed in her bed, filled with anguish. Finally, she slipped out bed and got down on her knees. There, she asked God to forgive her and to make "a manger in her heart" for Jesus. From that night on she understood that the Lord was with her in her trials, that He empathized with her in her sorrow, and that He had a plan for her life that would unfold as she walked with Him. She became an example of faith and grace that holds up in every circumstance.

Major League outfielder Todd Hollandsworth says, "I understand that everything that happens to me—everything I go through—is orchestrated, is something that God already knows. He knows yesterday, today, and tomorrow. I'm a firm believer that every day is granted to us. He is just so loving and so gracious."

Most sports fans are familiar with the story of Rams' quarterback Kurt Warner, who was overlooked by talent scouts for years. He wound up playing in the

Arena Football League, where he finally attracted enough attention that the Rams gave him a shot. All he did for the Rams was set all sorts of passing records en route to two Most Valuable Player awards and two Super Bowl appearances—one of which the Rams won.

Warner says now, "My story is about my faith in God and about how the Lord helped me get to this point. It wasn't being lucky or having all these bad breaks, and then finally getting a good break. It is about how the Lord used my whole situation and He built me up to where I could handle this. I could take hold of the success, and I could really take on responsibility for the position I had...the platform He gave me. I could use that to touch a lot of lives."

Todd Beamer perished when United Flight 93 crashed into a field in Pennsylvania on September 11, 2001. Even though he was only a young man with a wife and two small sons, it seems certain that part of God's plan for Todd's life was that he should help to steer that jetliner away from populated areas and thereby save hundreds or even thousands of lives. In the process of sacrificing his life to save others, Todd Beamer also showed the entire world what it means to have faith in God.

In a *Newsweek* article titled, "The Real Story of Flight 93," the American people learned about what happened during those final hours aboard the doomed airliner. The article says, "Todd had been afraid. More than once he called out for his Savior."

After the plane was taken over by terrorists, Beamer called the General Telephone Customer Service Center in Oak Brook, Illinois. He told Lisa Jefferson, the supervisor there, what was happening, explained that he and the other passengers were preparing to fight back, and asked her to pray with him.

"I don't think we're going to get out of this thing," he told her. "I'm going to have to go out on faith."

*Newsweek* tells us, "He began to recite the ancient litany, and Jefferson joined him: 'Our Father which art in heaven, Hallowed be thy name'" (Matthew 6:9 KJV). When they finished, Todd said, "Jesus, help me." Then he turned to the other passengers and asked if they were ready to go. When they responded in the affirmative, he said, "Let's roll!" A few minutes later the plane crashed, killing everyone on board.

Some people believe that Todd Beamer lost his life simply because he was in the wrong place at the wrong time. But I believe that, even though his death was a tragic loss, he was exactly where God wanted him to be. I am certain that, as soon as that airplane crashed, His Savior welcomed him into Paradise with open arms. His courage during the last terrible minutes of his life will stand as a tribute to Todd and his faith for generations to come.

I am certain that thousands of people have asked themselves, "What would I do if I found myself in a life-or-death situation like that? Would I face it with courage, or would I crumble into pieces?" I am also certain that hundreds, perhaps even thousands, of people have found the answers to their questions by surrendering their lives to the Lord Todd Beamer served.

It really is true that God has a plan for our lives, and His plan can be fulfilled in any circumstance in which we find ourselves. Of course, part of His plan is that we obey His moral laws. As James MacDonald says, these laws provide a pathway to get us safely "through the maze" of life. "Never do we have so much joy in this world as when we're living in conformity to God's Word. Never."

## God's Presence Will Bring You Joy

*"I will never leave you nor forsake you."*

—Joshua 1:5

Before I close this chapter on faith, I want to briefly tell you about two men. One of them has served God for his entire lifetime; the other turned his back on the Lord. The name of the first man is Billy Graham. Of course you know who he is, and I'll tell you more in just a moment.

The name of the second man is Charles Templeton. You have probably never heard of him. In the 1950s, both Billy Graham and Charles Templeton were becoming known around the world as dynamic young preachers. At the time, Templeton pastored a large church in Toronto and helped to found Youth for Christ in Canada.

Suddenly, at the height of his ministry, Templeton announced to the world that he had lost his faith. He simply turned his back on everything he had believed in and worked for and walked away. He became a successful newspaper editor, and even made a bid to become Canada's prime minister, but he never returned to the faith he had abandoned.

Author Lee Strobel went to Canada to interview Templeton for his book, *The Case for Faith*. He later wrote that Templeton still insists that He does not believe in "the God of the Old Testament." When Strobel asked him what he thought of Jesus, the ex-preacher, now in his eighties, bowed his head and began to cry. "I miss him," he wept.

Another writer, Joseph M. Stowell recently sat beside Billy Graham at a dinner in Fort Lauderdale, Florida. In the course of their conversation, he asked Dr. Graham what he had enjoyed most during his many years of preaching the Gospel. I'll let Stowell tell the story from here.

"Before he could answer, I suggested that perhaps it had been his times with and influence on presidents and heads of state. I was going to suggest that it might have been preaching the Gospel to great throngs around the world...Before I could go on, Graham said, with a determined softness in his voice, 'Beyond a doubt, it has been my fellowship with the Lord. To be able to talk with Him, to hear from Him, and to have His guidance and presence in my life has been my greatest joy.'"

Billy Graham is two years younger than Charles Templeton. In their younger days, they were friends who shared the ambition of spreading God's kingdom. As Stowell writes: "One man chose to stay with Jesus and, in his later years, he finds his greatest joy in the relationship that he has cultivated with Christ all through life. The other, having denied Jesus, in spite of a celebrated life, feels the loss deeply."

Faith, you see, will carry you through. Trust in Jesus and He will stay beside you, from now until the end of time.

CHAPTER FOURTEEN

# PUTTING IT ALL TOGETHER

*The key word is "respect."*
—Martin Luther King

During this journey together, we've talked at length about how scandal has rocked America's confidence in its major institutions over the last couple of decades. We have seen that this scandal is due largely to a turning away from godly morality. We've discussed the fact that, even though we may not be directly involved in scandalous behavior, we are all affected by it. What is more, as we return to a godly moral standard—or strengthen our adherence to a godly moral standard—we will change the society in which we live.

We started off by talking about some important concepts that we don't hear very much about nowadays.

- Having the right value system.
- Understanding that your life has a purpose.
- Being willing to do your duty.
- Being a person of virtue.
- Having high moral standards.

- Adhering to a well-defined standard of ethics.

- Being a person of honor.

- Striving to keep your reputation clean.

- Keeping your conscience tender and being willing to listen when it tells you that you're doing something wrong.

From this beginning, we went on to discuss the importance of becoming people who:

- Are always honest.

- Demonstrate integrity in all we do.

- Have a strong work ethic.

- Are mature.

- Are willing to take responsibility.

- Start, persevere, and finish.

- Are humble.

- Use influence wisely.

- Are courageous.

- Have faith in God.

Now I want to take a few minutes to talk about what happens when you incorporate all of these character traits into your life.

### You Become a Person People Respect

After Michael Jordan's last game in Orlando, on December 30, 2002, he took off his gray and white Nike shoes and handed them to the Magic's Tracy McGrady, with a message scribbled on the side: "Enjoyed the challenge. Good luck and stay healthy—*Michael Jordan.*" McGrady was floating on a cloud after a message of respect like that from MJ, arguably the best ever to play the game of basketball. But then again, McGrady was more than up to the challenge, scoring 32 points to lead the Magic to a 112-95 victory.

Having the respect of other people is tremendously important, but be aware that respect is not the same thing as fear. An employee may fear a boss who is a tyrant, but they will not respect them. A wife may meekly submit to a husband who is harsh, unyielding, and demanding, but she will not respect him. Children may act in a respectful manner toward abusive parents because they are afraid of being beaten, but this is not respect.

Proper respect involves admiration. It is shown in comments such as, "You can really count on that guy," or, "She's one of the finest people I know." If you live in a respectable way—that is, in line with the character traits we've discussed in this book—people will respect you. They may question you at first. They may even poke fun at you for a while and wonder why you don't join all the fun. However, as time goes by and they see your resolve to live a proper life, they will respect you, even if they don't want to!

Martin Luther King Jr. said, "Our lives begin to end the day we become silent about things that matter."

Author Denis Waitley says, "Understand that you yourself are no more than the composite picture of all your thoughts and actions. In your relationships with others, remember the basic and critically important rule: If you want to be loved, be lovable. If you want respect, set a respectable example."

Bill O'Reilly's recipe for respect is simply, "Always do what you say you are going to do. When you say that you are going to call someone back, you have to call that person back. When you promise to deliver a favor or perform a service, you must come through." He says that achieving respect "requires a consistency of behavior that is truly impressive. It requires that you treat others in an honest and caring way."

On the first day of training camp, Orlando Magic head coach Doc Rivers tells his players, "My only rule is respect. You respect your teammates, you respect the janitor, you respect everyone. If you do that, everything will be fine."

I also like this from Buck Rodgers, former manager of the California Angels: "There are countless ways of achieving greatness, but any road to achieving one's maximum potential must be built on a bedrock of respect for the individual, a commitment to excellence and a rejection of mediocrity." Or, as the great philosopher Goethe put it, "Treat people as if they were what they ought to be and you help them to become what they are capable of being."

I believe there are two important ways you can increase the respect other people have for you. They are:

- Respect other people.
- Respect yourself.

## Respect Other People

People who show respect for others generally get respect from others. Rich DeVos, my long-time mentor and boss, always showed respect for the people who worked for him. I've never forgotten what he once told me: "I built my whole (multi-billion-dollar) business on respect for people. I build them up; not chew them out. I always believe that if you show respect, you get respect." How true that has been. He is one of the most widely respected men I have ever known.

Baseball great Minnie Minoso, one of the sport's black pioneers, once said, "When you show respect for yourself and give it to others, the chances are great that you will get respect in return, no matter what your color or your origin. This has been my philosophy from day one."

In 1996 the Orlando Magic lost to the Chicago Bulls in the NBA's Eastern Conference playoffs. One afternoon before a game in Orlando, I had an opportunity to chat with Bulls' team physician John Hefferon. I asked him, "Twenty years from now, what do you suppose you'll remember most about Michael Jordan?"

He shook his head and said, "Aside from the fact that he's the most intense, competitive human being I've ever met and has no fear of failure...I think that what I'll remember most is that he treated everyone the same. From the president to the ball boy, from the Pope to the equipment manager, he treated everybody with respect."

Sandra L. Vivas is executive director of the American Volleyball Coaches Association. She says that the best investment she ever made was spending two years selling hotdogs at a concession stand in Dodger Stadium. "I learned, very quickly, how perception is reality: The public does not look very highly on those selling hot dogs, no matter one's background or education. It was a daily lesson in the subtleties of management (along with a dose of humility)."

What was the Number One lesson she learned during her time at the ballpark? "Treat everyone with dignity, no matter what their position in an organization. After all, if you lose your key to the gym, only the janitor can let you in." Or, as the apostle Paul put it: "God has combined the members of the body and has given greater honor to the parts that lacked it, so that there should be no division in the body, but that its parts should have equal concern for each other" (1 Corinthians 12:24-25).

When Thomas Jefferson was vice president of the United States, he arrived in Baltimore late one afternoon after spending the entire day on horseback. Dirty and exhausted, he went to the town's largest hotel and asked for a room. The proprietor took one look at the bedraggled man standing in front of him and said, in a haughty tone, "We have no room for you, Sir."

Without protesting Jefferson turned around, strode out of the hotel, and headed for another inn nearby. As he walked out the door, someone recognized him and told the proprietor that he had made a terrible mistake in turning Jefferson away. He immediately ordered his servants to follow the vice president, offer his deepest apologies, and bring him back to the hotel.

When they found Jefferson and gave him the message from their employer, he replied, "If he has no room for a dirty farmer, he shall have none for the vice-president." Jefferson, who wrote the words, "All men are created equal," would not stay in an establishment that did not demonstrate respect for all. He obviously believed, as did Albert Schweitzer, that "only those who respect others can be of real use to them."

## Respect Yourself

No matter who you are, if you show that you respect yourself, other people will also respect you. From the time I was a young boy I made up my mind that I would not smoke, drink, or carouse. Even in college, I was never tempted to go against what I knew was right. However, I certainly took a lot of ragging for my morality. Even so, I learned quickly that even though they teased me, my buddies really did respect me and the stand I was taking. You see, you don't have to preach or pontificate. If you simply show by your actions that you're going to stand up for what is right, they will respect you. They may not tell you flat out, "I respect you," but they'll show you that they do.

I know some very talented people who go around bashing themselves all the time. One woman told me, "I'd rather laugh at my own expense than at someone else's expense." That's an admirable motivation, I suppose, but why should we have to laugh at *anyone's* expense? Being able to laugh at yourself is a good thing, but if you constantly put yourself down and don't seem to respect yourself, other people will just naturally start to think that you're not worthy of their respect either. I agree with the great novelist Fyodor Dostoyevsky, who said, "If you want to be respected by others, the great thing is to respect yourself."

Brian Tracy, whom I have quoted many times throughout this book, says, "There is a direct relationship between your own level of self-esteem and the health of your personality. The more you like and respect yourself, the more you like and respect other people. The more you consider yourself to be a valuable and worthwhile person, the more you consider others to be valuable and worthwhile as well. The more you accept yourself just as you are, the more you accept others just as they are."

For years Dr. Benjamin Spock was America's foremost authority on parenting. He advised parents, "Respect children, but ask for respect from your children also. Trust yourself. You know more than you think you do."

If you are ever tempted to get down on yourself, remember that God loves you so much that He sent His only Son to die on your behalf. I am convinced that if you were the only person on this whole planet who had ever sinned, God would have sent His Son for you alone! How can you not respect yourself if God sees you as that valuable?

Writer Hal Urban says, "Good people build their lives on a foundation of respect." Then he goes on to give seven rewards that come from showing respect to others:

- We develop effective social skills and habits.
- We make other people feel good.
- We earn the respect of others.
- We establish good relationships.
- We are treated better by other people.
- We improve our feelings of self-worth.
- We build a solid foundation.

## You Become a Person of Trust

*Few delights can equal the mere presence*
*of one whom we trust, utterly.*
—George MacDonald, Author

Trust is at the heart of all good relationships. You might say that trust is the glue that binds people together. It is a high compliment indeed when others describe you as someone who can be trusted.

The other night I was watching *Monday Night Football* when broadcaster Al Michaels described a deceptive statement from a football coach as "Clinton-speak." When I heard that, I thought about how sad it was that

Bill Clinton tainted his legacy by not being trustworthy. The American people thought enough of Clinton that they re-elected him in a landslide. However, twenty years from now I wonder if he will be remembered more for the things he accomplished as president or for lying about his relationship with Monica Lewinsky.

Writer Jamie Clarke says, "Once trust is lost in any relationship, it is like a mirror struck by a stone. The glass shatters, and although tiny pieces can be glued back into position, the mirror always shows the cracks. They are deep and numerous."

I also like this from Dr. Marilyn Mason: "Trust is primary to any relationship. It is the covenant of commitment. I use the word 'covenant' because of the sense of solemnity generated by our putting total reliance—some would call it faith—in the space between ourselves and others."

In Francis Fukiyama's book, *Trust*, he presents evidence that a high level of trust even helps nations become more prosperous. His research has shown that "high-trust nations" are generally prosperous and offer greater opportunities for more and more people, whereas "low-trust nations" have lower levels of prosperity and development.

When there is more trust among the people, the government, and the business community, there is a higher level of economic activity, growth, economic development, and thus prosperity. When there is a low level of trust, and thus a higher level of corruption and dishonesty, people are reluctant to invest in their country's economy. This lack of trust results in a low level of economic activity, slow growth, almost no development, and poverty.

Trust builds. Lack of trust destroys; whether we are talking about the health of a nation's economy or the health of a relationship between two people. We've certainly seen evidence of this in America. When consumer confidence was shaken by all the scandals in the corporate world, the stock market plunged. Only when the breech of trust is repaired will the market begin to approach its previous levels.

Brian Tracy says, "Trust is the foundation of all relationships. When people feel they can trust you to keep your word and to do what you say you will do, they will give you greater responsibilities. When people feel they will be more successful getting the things they want by relying on you, they will open countless doors for you."

Of course, it's also important that you and I demonstrate an attitude of trust toward others. If you trust other people, you will be let down from time to time; but an occasional disappointment, as painful as it might be, is much better than closing yourself off and refusing to trust anybody. When people know that you trust them, it means more to them than you can possibly know. It makes them feel good about themselves and gives them the strength they need to live up to your expectations.

If you are a boss or a company owner, it's important to show your employees that you trust them to do a good job for you. If you are an employee, it's important to show your boss that you trust that they will make wise decisions that will benefit you. If you are a parent, it is important to show your children that you trust them. Remember now, I have nineteen children, so I know from experience what I'm talking about!

I am not talking about being reckless or trusting people who have proven that they aren't worthy of being trusted. It would be ridiculous for a mother to find drug paraphernalia in her teenager's bedroom and then say, "Oh well, I trust you." And it certainly wasn't the best thing for Enron's employees to have trusted their company's leadership. What I am talking about is trust that always gives other people the benefit of the doubt, trust that expects the best from others and considers them innocent until and unless they prove themselves guilty.

Robert Galvin, who went on to become chief operating officer of Motorola, says that when he was a child, "My father imposed on me the greatest discipline. He trusted me." In many ways, when you trust other people, you set them free to soar.

Ralph Waldo Emerson was very close to the mark when he wrote, "Trust men and they will be true to you. Treat them greatly, and they will show themselves great." It doesn't always work out that way, but I'd say from my own experience that fewer than 10 percent of the people you trust will let you down. (And it's probably much lower than that.)

Writer Stephen Ambrose had a way of making history come alive. Here is what he had to say about former President Dwight Eisenhower: "When associates described Eisenhower, be they superiors or subordinates, there was one word that almost all of them used. It was trust. People trusted Eisenhower for the most obvious reason: he was trustworthy. Disagree as they might (and often did) with his decisions, they never doubted his motives...With his staff and with his troops, with his superiors and with his subordinates, as with foreign governments, Eisenhower did what he said he was going to do. His reward was the trust placed in him."

Ambrose goes on to say that the selection of Eisenhower as supreme commander, Allied Expeditionary Force, was "quite possibly the best appointment (President Franklin) Roosevelt ever made." Trust is so very important!

Here's another story about another great man from America's past who also gained the trust of others. His name was Albert Einstein. The brilliant scientist was on a passenger train heading out of New York City when he realized he'd lost his ticket. By the time the conductor reached his seat, Einstein had turned all of his pants pockets inside out and was frantically digging through his briefcase looking for that ticket.

"Don't worry, Mr. Einstein," the conductor said. "I recognize you, and I trust you. You don't have to give me your ticket."

Einstein didn't respond. He continued to rummage through items in his briefcase.

"Really, sir," the conductor offered again. "It's all right. I trust you."

Einstein, widely regarded as the best mind of his time, looked up with a perturbed expression on his face. "Young man," he said. "This is not a matter of trust. It's a matter of direction. I have no idea where I'm going!"

Well, I guess you do have to have a *few* other things along with trust!

In addition to trusting others, it's also important to trust God in every situation—and especially when it seems things aren't going the way you want them to go. Rick Warren says, "I must choose to obey God in faith. Every time you trust God's wisdom and do whatever He says, even when you don't understand it, you deepen your friendship with God."

Chuck Swindoll builds on this when he writes, "God has trusted each of us with our own set of unfair circumstances and unexplained experiences to deal with. Can we still trust in Him, even if He never tells us why? The secret to responsible trust is acceptance. Acceptance is taking from God's hand absolutely anything He gives, looking into His face in trust and thanksgiving, knowing that the confinement of the hedge we're in is good and for His glory."

I also love this from writer/speaker Beth Moore: "The prescription for worry is trust. Trust comes to those who take God at His Word. Make a list of all your reasons to worry; then write the word TRUST in big, bold letters on top of your list; then, seek Him and seek His kingdom with everything you've got...and all the right things will be given to you as well (see Matthew 6:33)."

Speaking of lists, if you were to write the names of all the people you trust, who would be on that list? Your spouse? Your parents? Your brother or sister? Your best friend? A more important question is, if all the people you know wrote out a Most-Trusted List, how many of them would include your name? An admirable goal would be to get your name on as many of those lists as possible.

In their book, *God's Vitamin C for the Spirit*, Kathy Collard Miller and D. Larry Miller tell about a group of botanists who found an extremely rare plant growing high in the Alps. Their excitement over their discovery was cooled by the fact that the plant was growing out of the side of a steep precipice. They couldn't possibly reach it without putting their lives at risk. They were not experienced mountain climbers, and none of them were familiar with the terrain.

Then they hit upon an idea. A small boy was watching some sheep nearby. They could attach a lifeline to the boy and lower him down to the plant, so he could snip off a small specimen. They approached him, explained what they wanted, and told him they'd give him several gold coins for helping them out.

The shepherd boy wanted those coins, but it was a long, long way down to that plant, and he wasn't sure he could trust the strangers to hold that rope. But just think of what he could buy with that money! Suddenly, he had a brilliant idea. He told the botanists that if they could wait for a few minutes, he'd be right back to help them.

He ran off toward the small village in the nearby valley. Within five minutes, he was back, walking hand-in-hand with an older man. "All right," he announced, "You can tie the rope under my arms now. I'll go into the canyon, as long as you let my father hold the rope."

We can trust our mothers and fathers because we know how very much they love us. They'll do anything they can to prevent bad things from happening to us. Isn't it great that we have a Heavenly Father who loves us even more than our earthly parents do? After all, God's love is infinite, boundless—and we are part of His family! The apostle John wrote, "How great is the love the Father has lavished on us, that we should be called the children of God! And that is what we are!" (1 John 3:1).

So far in this chapter, we've seen that when you are a person of character, you will gain respect and trust. Another thing that happens is:

**You Become a Person Who Inspires Loyalty in Others**

*You can buy a man's time. You can buy a man's physical presence in a given place. You can even buy a*

*number of skilled, muscular, motions each day. But you*
*cannot buy enthusiasm and loyalty. You must earn these.*
—Clarence Francis,
Former Chairman of General Foods

R. E. Littlejohn, who gave me one of my first jobs in sports at Spartanburg, South Carolina, taught me a lesson about loyalty that I'll never forget. After the 1965 baseball season, the radio station that carried our games fired John Gordon, our play-by-play announcer. John was a friend of mine, so I was pretty upset, but I figured there wasn't anything I could do about it.

Mr. Littlejohn felt differently. He called a meeting with the station owner, and that was the first—and last—time I ever saw him get really angry. When the station owner wouldn't rehire Gordon, Littlejohn said, "Then we'll find another station." And he wasn't bluffing. Even though we had a profitable relationship with our current station, we "fired" them.

As it turned out, we moved to a stronger station, our ratings went up during a championship year, and John Gordon continued as the team's announcer for four more years. I think all of these things happened directly because of Mr. Littlejohn's loyalty. Today John Gordon is the respected radio voice of the Minnesota Twins, and I'm sure he would be the first to tell you that he owes some of his success to the loyalty demonstrated by R.E. Littlejohn so many years ago!

What exactly is loyalty? In his book, *Hanging by a Thread*, Mark Rutland puts it this way: "Loyalty never usurps authority. It refuses to accept inappropriate love or praise that might properly exalt another. Loyalty is the glue that holds relationships together, makes families functional and armies victorious. Loyalty is the fabric of society. Without loyalty, no enlisted man can dare to hope that his general cares whether he lives or dies. No captain can expect an inconvenient order to be obeyed. Without loyalty, marriage becomes a competitive minefield. Companies become dangerously paranoid."

As you put these character traits into play, people will respect you. You become a person people can trust. And when the members of a unit are loyal to each other, there's no limit to what they can accomplish.

To my knowledge there has never been a sports team as successful as the old Boston Celtics. Beginning in the mid-1950s and lasting for about thirty years, they were dominant. When a reporter asked Boston's legendary coach, Red Auerbach, why the team had been so successful, he said, "Loyalty is a two-way street." In other words, the Celtics were able to get the best basketball players because those players knew they would be treated fairly in Boston. Auerbach made sure that his players knew the Celtics organization cared about them, on and off the court. They were viewed as people and not just as basketball players.

Writer Alan Webber said, "Players wanted to play in Boston; not only because they knew they could win games, but because they knew they would be appreciated and valued." Auerbach's treatment of his players reminds me of something General George S. Patton said: "There is a great deal of talk about loyalty from the bottom to the top. Loyalty from the top down is even more necessary and much less prevalent."

I also agree with former New York Mayor Rudy Giuliani, who says that loyalty should be "established as a culture" throughout any organization. He writes, "Any large group is bound to have intramural rivalries and, if people are talented and driven, a number of them will think they're the smartest in the room. To a degree, that's a good thing. Competition often brings out the best. When competitive rivalries turn to sniping, however, a leader has to remind everyone that they are all working toward the same ultimate goals."

Are there some specific things you can do to help create loyalty in others? Absolutely! You can:

- Be loyal to them.

- Show them that you are genuinely interested in them as people, and not just because they can benefit you in some way.

- Listen when they talk. As theologian Paul Tillich said, "The first duty of love is to listen."

- Deal with them openly, honestly, and fairly.

- Be an encourager.

- Give credit where credit is due.

Author Mark McCormack writes, "In my mind loyalty is the greatest virtue." Close, but not quite. There's an even greater virtue. And that brings me to the fourth and final blessing that comes to people of character.

## You Will Be Loved and Be Able to Love Others

Love. That's the greatest character trait of all. The Number One antidote to scandal and corruption.

I've been talking quite a bit about my boss, Rich DeVos—and there's a reason for that. I have never known another man of his stature who is beloved by so many people. Everyone who knows him absolutely loves him! It is a truly remarkable thing to see. Being loved like this and being able to give back love in return is truly what life is all about, and it is the end result of living a life of character.

Rich answers all of his own mail—an incredible amount of correspondence—usually with a handwritten note. He always ends each note the same way, even to people he doesn't know: "Love ya! Rich." This is so typical of the man.

It reminds me of an article I saw recently about the death of Sid Gillman, a man who played such an important role in the development of the National Football League. Dick Vermeil, who is now head coach of the Kansas City Chiefs, said, "I don't think I've ever had a phone call from him (Sid) that didn't finish with him saying, 'Hey, I love you, Dick.'" What a great way to be remembered!

Earlier I mentioned Buck O'Neal, the ninety-one-year-old gentleman who was such a great baseball player in the old Negro Leagues. When O'Neal was asked by reporter Steve Rushin to give the secret behind his long, happy life, O'Neal replied, "Love, man. Love is the whole thing."

I agree with former British Prime Minister Benjamin Disraeli, who said, "We are all born for love. It is the principle of existence and its only end." Willa Cather wrote, "When there is great love, there are always miracles." And the apostle Paul tells us, "And now these three remain: faith, hope and love. But the greatest of these is love" (1 Corinthians 13:13).

When Jesus was asked which commandment was the greatest of all, He said, "'Love the Lord your God with all your heart and with all your soul and with all your mind.' This is the first and greatest commandment. And the second is like it: 'Love your neighbor as yourself.' All the Law and the Prophets hang on these two commandments" (Matthew 22:37-40).

A person who loves God, others, and self, will just naturally be honest, kind, loyal and, in fact, demonstrate all of the other character traits we have been talking about throughout this book. It can work the other way too. A person who practices being honest, who has high moral standards, who is humble, who is loyal, who demonstrates all of the other character traits we have talked about, will grow into a person who loves and is loved. As Victor Hugo said, "The supreme happiness of life is that we are loved."

When I was going through a down time in my life, a friend advised me, "Act as if you're cheerful, and pretty soon you will be." It sounded silly, but it worked for me. In the same way, if you act as if your heart is full of love—even when it's not—pretty soon it will be! That's why I try to do as radio talk show host Delilah suggests in her book, *Love Someone Today*: "When you reach out in love and build someone up, you usually end up building yourself up as well. Whether it is something as fleeting as a warm smile or holding a door open for an elderly person or sacrificing your seat on a crowded subway so a tired mother can sit with her child, a small act of kindness goes a long way."

Dr. Barbara DeAngelis said, "Love is a force more formidable than any other. It is invisible...it cannot be seen or measured; yet, it is powerful enough to transform you in a moment and offer you more joy than material possession could."

Just in case you are tempted to think that the notion of love is an illogical or abstract notion that doesn't apply to life in the real world; Herb Kelleher, CEO of Southwest Airlines, says, "We'd rather have a company run by love; not by fear." Southwest Airlines even calls its company newsletter Luv Lines. Do you suppose it's a coincidence that Southwest is booming while other airlines are struggling to survive?

Ben Cohen of Ben & Jerry's Ice Cream feels as Kelleher does. He says, "When you give love, you receive love." He adds, "There is a spiritual dimension to business, just as there is to the lives of individuals."

Another who believes in love's importance is Pamela Coker, CEO of a successful software company, Acucobol. "Love your customers, employees, shareholders, vendors, and community," she says, "and the profits will follow." She also says, "I am committed to helping every Acucobol employee achieve his or her dreams."

Meanwhile, over at Gore-Tex, Chief Financial Officer Shanti Mehta says that company was built on love. Speaking of company Founder Bill Gore, Mehta says, "He never called me into his office. He always came to my desk...He was a real well-spring from which love flowed throughout the organization...After his death, the responsibility of doing this has fallen squarely on the shoulders of us all."

This is as it should be. The responsibility to love does fall squarely on the shoulders of us all.

It is said that near the end of his life, the apostle John came to Rome to speak to the believers there. Thousands gathered to hear the last survivor of the original Twelve Apostles—this man who had actually known the Lord, had witnessed His miracles, heard His voice, and stood awestruck in the empty tomb. By this time John was bent with age and his hair completely silver. When the time came for him to speak, he had to be helped out of his chair and stood before the congregation trembling with palsy.

The congregation grew deathly quiet. No one wanted to miss a single word of what would surely be John's final message to the Church. Certainly, he had given much thought and preparation to his final remarks.

They were sure to be of the utmost importance. "My little children," he began, in a voice that rang with clarity and authority. "Love one another." Then he sat down, his sermon finished.

I can think of no more important words to leave with you today. There is nothing more important, stronger, or greater than love. Let us love one another because: *Love is the power that can change our communities, our nation, and our world.*

Always remember: God loves you and so do I!

# Afterword

Between the time I finished writing the last chapter of this book and it was prepared to go to press, our nation continued to be hit by scandal upon scandal upon scandal. There were so many scandals, in fact, that most of them were no longer considered to be front-page news. Instead, they were buried somewhere in Section D of most daily newspapers.

When I first sat down to write *American Scandal*, I thought, "Wouldn't it be wonderful if everything had changed by the time I finished?" I would have gladly thrown this entire manuscript into the nearest trash can if I could have sensed that it was no longer needed. How I wish there had been a revival of character that made it obsolete.

Sadly, that hasn't happened.

Instead, over the next few weeks:

- In Washington, officials of a teachers' union have been accused of stealing more than $5 million from members' dues. They allegedly used the money to buy things like designer clothes and fur coats.

- A few days later, word came that a once-huge company named National Century Financial Enterprises was going out of business...in the midst of a federal investigation into accounting irregularities.

- Meanwhile, from upstate New York, USA Today reported that, "The president of St. Bonaventure University resigned after a tumultuous week for the school's men's basketball program, one of several scandals that have rocked the sport in recent days." The newspaper reported that the school's athletic director and two coaches had been placed on administrative leave pending further investigation.

- And down South at the University of Georgia, head coach Jim Harrick resigned, and his son, Jim Jr., was fired amid allegations of misconduct. Allegedly, Harrick Jr. handed out some grades to basketball players who took a course he taught. What was wrong? Allegedly no classes were ever held, and students were never asked to do any work.

- This one from the New York Times: "The nations' largest chain of rehabilitation hospitals was accused (by the securities and exchange commission) of sweeping

accounting fraud stretching back to its
inception in a case that regulators say
may rival the wrong doing at Enron and
WorldCom." Later, federal prosecutors
said the hospital chain HealthSouth
faked $1.1 billion in profits in 1997 and
1990. This is in addition to $1.4 billion
in false profits reported since 1999. In-
vestigators found that employees were
ordered to falsity reports to meet budg-
etary projections. Eleven top executives
have pleaded guilty.

How did we ever get so far from godly principles—
such as those espoused by men like Henry Clay? He
said, "Of all the properties which belong to honorable
men, not one is so highly prized as that of character."
And James Cash Penney, founder of the department
store chain that bears his name said, "Golden-Rule
principles are just as necessary for operating a business
as trucks, typewriters or twine."

Marianne Jennings, a professor at Arizona State University, uses the term "ethics creep" to explain how so
many American businesses got so far off track. She says
that some business leaders kept taking small liberties,
tiny steps over the "ethics line," and eventually found
themselves engaged in full-blown corruption. Authors
Carolyn B. Thompson and James W. Ware explain it
this way: "This is similar to the well-known study in
which frogs are placed in a pot of water that is then
slowly heated. The frogs never jump out, because the increase in temperature is so gradual, and eventually they

are boiled to death. Likewise, leaders who get scaled in their own ethical waters often express disbelief at what has happened. 'How did it go this far?' they wonder. Same way—a gradual increase in "temperature.'"

As Chuck Colson said on his "Breakpoint" radio broadcast, "We can only begin to deal with the moral malaise in American life when we begin to cultivate personal virtue."

It is time to call America back to the principles that made her great!

It is time to remember that, as Chuck Colson said, "The one real answer to our moral malaise and the crumbling confidence in American business does not come through laws or statutes or better social conditions. Just as the Bible has been telling us all along, it comes through personal righteousness."

Over the next few pages, I want to briefly review the building blocks to moral character we talked about in the *American Scandal*, beginning with:

### Honesty

I recently came across a study undertaken at the Center for Creative Leadership in Greensboro, North Carolina, in which it was determined that, "the best predictor of success in an organization is leadership that behaves with integrity and honesty."

Ron Dittemore was thrust into the national spotlight in a very tragic way. The manager of NASA's Space Shuttle program was introduced to most of us when the shuttle Columbia exploded upon re-entry into the earth's atmosphere. As I watched news coverage of the shuttle disaster, I was impressed by Dittemore's forthrightness with reporters. His answers were straightforward and direct. That's why I wasn't surprised to read this assessment by Eugene Kranz, a former colleague at NASA: "He (Dittemore) is the epitome of the leader who knows the buck stops with him. He knows that the only way you survive is through absolute, ruthless, honesty." This is something I wish everyone understood.

The next building block is always "doing the right thing," or, in other words:

## Integrity

I love this quote from CBS-television sports announcer Clark Kellogg, commenting on the state of college basketball in 2003: "You can't legislate morality. It's a heart issue. Do you want to do what's right, or do you want to get beyond by doing what's wrong? Do you want to buy a trophy or do you want to earn it?"

Dr. Billy Graham put it this way: "Some of the greatest gifts that God gives a person is the ability to lie down at night satisfied with who he is and what he has done that day because he has acted with integrity."

The next building block is:

## Hard Work

Baseball great Pete Rose has been in the news lately, because of talk that he is going to be "forgiven" by Major League Baseball. If you're a sports fan you know that Rose is not in baseball's Hall of Fame—nor is he allowed to participate in Major League Baseball in any way—because he allegedly wagered on baseball games while he was playing and coaching. (Rose has always denied these allegations, by the way.) But even though there have been questions about Rose's ethics, nobody had ever questioned his work ethic.

Former teammate Jim Kaat shakes his head with amazement as he remembers a game in which Rose, uncharacteristically, didn't get a base hit. Afterwards, while the rest of the players showered, dressed and left the stadium, Rose was back down on the field, with one of the coaches.

"It was past 11 p.m.," Kaat remembers, "and he was taking batting practice!"

No wonder Peter Rose went on to become Major League Baseball's all-time hits leader. Hard work always pays off.

The next building block is:

### Maturity

Here's what author David Frum has to say about the mature attitude displayed by President George W. Bush:

"He is a man of ferocious self-discipline. He is in amazing physical condition. His eating regime is very strict. You can also see it in the way he speaks; he thinks very hard about what he is going to say. This is a man under great self-control."

Like cream in milk, invariably, the person with the mature, self-controlled attitude is the one who rises to the top.

In Chapter Eight, we talked about the importance of:

## Responsibility

Much too often these days, people try to find someone else to blame for all their problems. The other day, I saw a television commercial for a law firm that specializes in personal injury cases. "If you've been hurt in an accident," the commercial promised, "we can get you money. Even if the accident was your fault." What a sad comment on modern American society.

Recently, a couple in New York City sued McDonald's for contributing to their two teenage daughters' obesity and other health problems. I was delighted when I read the ruling issued by U.S. District Court Judge Robert Sweet. He asked, "Where should the line be drawn between an individual's own responsibility to take care of herself and society's responsibility to ensure others shield her? The complaint fails to allege the McDonald's products consumed by the plaintiffs were dangerous in any other way than that which was reasonable and oblivious to a reasonable consumer."

Bravo! Anyone who eats a steady diet of McDonald's cheeseburgers is probably going to get fat! That shouldn't be a surprise to anyone. Someone who smokes for 25 years is probably going to get lung cancer or heart disease. That shouldn't be a surprise either.

If you don't want to become obese, eat right and exercise. If you want to avoid tobacco-related illnesses, don't smoke. It's really that simple.

A strong, healthy American society will be one in which we all take responsibility for our own actions.

In Chapter Nine, we talked about:

## Starting, Persevering, and Finishing

In other words, never giving up.

That reminds me of a great quote from former heavyweight boxing champion Jack Dempsey: "A champion is one who gets up when he can't."

I'd say that explains it pretty well!

Next on the list is:

## Humility

President George W. Bush said: "I've never held myself out to be any great genius."

When you really have confidence in yourself, it's easy to be humble. When you understand that God has a plan for your life, and that you are important to Him, you don't have to go around bragging about yourself and showing other people how important you are. As I've traveled through life, I've met some arrogant, self-important people. (Haven't we all!) But I don't let them make me angry. Instead, I feel sorry for them. After all, if your own reflection is all you can see, you're missing a lot of beautiful things in this world!

The next building block is:

## Using Your Influence Wisely

That reminds me of a story about Major League Baseball's slugger Jim Thome, who now plays for the Philadelphia Phillies. Hal Bodley writes that Thome was a Cub's fan growing up in Central Illinois. He especially idolized Dave (Kong) Kingman, who was known for his towering home runs.

One day, when Jim was eight, his dad took him to Wrigley Field to see the Cubs play baseball. While they were there, he tried to get his hero to autograph a baseball, but "Kong" walked right past him. His dad told reporter Bodley, "Before I knew what happened, my son had disappeared. Moments later, I spotted him in the Cub's dugout, and he still had that ball in his hand." He didn't get Kingman's autograph, although some other Cub's players signed a baseball for him.

The senior Thome says that the incident at Wrigley Field gave his son a lesson he will always remember. "He's never forgotten how hurt he was, and I know he'll never treat anybody like that."

It is important to do as political leader Susanna Agnelli advises: "People will run after you when they think you are important, so keep your feet on the ground."

Next building block:

## Courage

On February 1, 2003, the space shuttle Columbia disintegrated upon re-entry into the earth's atmosphere. Our entire nation was shaken by that terrible tragedy. Yet the disaster also served as a much-needed reminder of the courage that has enabled America to become a world leader in every area of endeavor—space exploration, science, medicine, computer technology, athletics, literature, business, etc.

Immediately following the Columbia's loss, Peggy Noonan wrote: "We forget to notice the everyday courage of astronauts. We forget to think about all the Americans doing big and dangerous things...members of the armed forces, cops and firemen, doctors in public hospitals in hard places."

We have all benefited from the courage of others. So let us strive to be courageous.

It is important to remember as we go through life that achievement goes hand-in-hand with courage. As President George W. Bush has said, "Great endeavors are inseparable from great risks."

We recently saw an incredible example of courage during Operation Iraqi Freedom. It started when 19-year-old Army supply clerk Jessica Lynch became involved in a fire fight with Iraqi soldiers. Although vastly outnumbered, and severely injured, she continued to fire her rifle until her ammunition ran out. Finally, she was captured and ended up in a Baghdad hospital.

There, a 32-year-old Iraqi lawyer named Mohammed—we didn't know his last name until later—couldn't bear to see the way she was being treated. Although he knew he was putting his own life at risk—as well as the lives of everyone in his family—he walked six miles through the desert to report Private Lynch's location to American troops.

Almost immediately, a daring rescue operation was put into action. Heavily armed Marines surrounded the hospital, while Navy Seals went inside and brought their captured comrade out on a stretcher. Meanwhile, the Air Force stood by to assist if necessary.

What a wonderful display of courage—on the part of Jessica Lynch, Mohammed, and all those involved in the rescue operation. May God grant us all such courage in difficult circumstances!

The next building block to a strong moral character, and thus, a strong moral society, is:

## Faith

A moment ago, I mentioned the great courage of all those who died in the explosion of the space shuttle Columbia. Now I want to talk about one reason why Commander Rick Husband—and at least two other members of his crew—were able to have such courage: He had a personal relationship with the One who holds the entire universe in His hands. He knew that whatever happened, nothing could take them out of the safety provided by God's constant love and care.

Before leaving on his final flight, Commander Husband put together seventeen videos for each of his two children so they could have private devotions together while he was away. Just before the crew boarded the Columbia, he prayed out loud for them. Later, one of the crew members remarked that he had never heard of a commander praying for his flight crew before a flight.

Rick Husband's prayers did not cause the shuttle disaster to be averted. But because of his faith, he had the assurance that his soul would never die. He knew that as soon as his physical body was dead, his soul would be at home with Jesus.

All human beings have to die someday. Faith in God won't protect you from that—nor will it keep trouble away from you. But faith will sustain you and keep you no matter what else may happen.

Norm Evans, who once played football for the Miami Dolphins, said, "What I want people to realize is that success in sports or in the world's eyes pales in comparison to the incredible, long-lasting, on-going, every-growing relationship that you can have with God through Jesus Christ."

What happens when you surrender your life to Christ? Someone has said that it is like being a pumpkin that God picks out of the patch. "He brings you in and washes all the dirt off you. Then he cuts off the top and scoops out all the yucky stuff. He removes the seeds of doubt, hate, greed, etc. Then he carves you a new smiling face and puts the light inside of you to shine for all the world to see."

Every heart needs to have the light of God inside it. If you take with you only one lesson from this book, I hope it is that a right relationship with God is the number one answer to all of our problems. I like the way University of Nebraska assistant football coach Ron

Brown put it: "When you squeeze God out of the equation, you will get mass chaos. If you squeeze God out of your heart, you will get personal chaos."

### True Integrity Is a Supernatural Trait

Never forget that God loves you, that He wants the best for you, and He is always there to create the individual you and I are meant to be. As he says, "Fear not, for I am with you, be not dismayed, for I am your God; I will strengthen you, I will help you, I will uphold you with my victorious hand: (Is. 41:10 RSV).

# ABOUT THE AUTHOR

You can contact Pat Williams directly at:

Pat Williams
c/o The Orlando Magic
8701 Maitland Summit Boulevard
Orlando, FL 32810

(407) 916-2404
pwilliams@orlandomagic.com

If you would like to set up a speaking engagement for Pat Williams,

> please call or write his assistant, Melinda Ethington, at the above address, or call her at (407) 916-2454.

> Requests can also be faxed to (407) 916-2986 or e-mailed to methington@orlandomagic.com.